REPUBLICANS

DO THE DUMBEST THINGS

REPUBLICANS

DO THE DUMBEST THINGS™

Bill Crawford

RENAISSANCE BOOKS

Los Angeles

Library of Congress Catalog Card Number: 00-101345
ISBN: 1-58063-111-8

10 9 8 7 6 5 4 3

Design by Lee Fukui

Published by Renaissance Books
Distributed by St. Martin's Press
Manufactured in the United States of America
First Edition

Dedicated to the
wisdom (and patience) of
the American voter

Acknowledgments

Thanks to my coauthor "Deep Throat," who wishes to remain anonymous; Mitch Blank and Arlete Santos at Archive Photos, Holly Jones at AP/World Wide photos, Andy "Wild Turkey" McCord, my agent Jim "the Bookworm" Hornfischer, my editor James Robert Parish, my grammatical guru Allan Taylor, and all the folks at Renaissance Books. Also, special thanks to Frank Smejkal for creating and maintaining the dumbest site on the Web: www.dumbest.com.

Thanks to the following for help with photos: Steve Branch, Ronald Reagan Library; Debbie Bush, George Bush Presidential Library; Kenneth G. Hafeli, Gerald R. Ford Library; Tom House, Ohio State Historical Society; Heather Moore, Historical Office, Office of the Secretary, United States Senate; Nixon Project, National Archives.

Special thanks to Amelia, Diana, Joe, and Gene "Big Daddy of Border Radio" Fowler. Gene, you're the ram-what-am-with-every-lamb.

CONTENTS

The Third-Party Politicians

INTRODUCTION

Republicans do the dumbest things. Just ask any Democrat. And vice versa. "The more you read and observe about this politics thing," Will Rogers, the revered sage of Oklahoma, once noted, "you got to admit that each party is worse than the other."

Writer Ambrose Bierce defined politics as "the conduct of public affairs for private advantage." Perhaps it is too harsh to say that every politician is corrupt. Napoleon Bonaparte was probably more accurate when he declared centuries ago, "In politics stupidity is not a handicap."

Stupidity, what an advantage! As Americans, we have come to expect politicians to do the dumbest things, and, generally, they have never let us down. For over two hundred years, we often have cast our votes for deadbeats, hypocrites, bigots, womanizers, drunks, and slobs, as well as good-hearted men and women who for some strange reason got into politics.

Are Republicans any dumber than Democrats? I believe this question should be answered by a vote. Check out what America thinks at our Web site (www.dumbest.com) and vote for yourself.

Are politicians less swift than other breeds of celebrities? As the coauthor of *Movie Stars Do the Dumbest Things*, I have to agree with the celebrated actor Spencer Tracy who growled once, "Acting is not the noblest profession in the world, but there are things lower than acting—not many, mind you—but politicians give you something to look down on from time to time."

Compiling the present volume has been a humbling experience. "There is no credit to being a comedian when you have the whole government working for you," Will Rogers once admitted. "All you have to do is report the facts."

Indeed: Truth is dumber than fiction.

KEY TO ENTRIES

I have restricted the entries in this book to politicians who have run for federal office (the U.S. House of Representatives, the U.S. Senate, or president of the United States), or for governor of a particular state. In the Local Loonies chapter, I have included some Republicans who ran for other state and local offices.

Politicians are identified as Pres. (President, if only the person's last name is cited), Rep. (Representative, if only the person's last name is used) for a member of the U.S. House of Representatives, Sen. (Senator, if only the person's last name is used) for a member of the U.S. Senate, or Gov. (Governor, if only the person's last name is used) for a state governor.

DUMBEST QUOTE

Lists the dumbest quote or quotes spoken by the Republican. When necessary for clarity, the quote is identified by year and/or circumstance.

FACTS OF LIFE (and Death)

ORIGIN: Gives the full name, place of birth, date of birth, and (where appropriate) the date, place, and, if known, cause of death of the Republican.

FORMATIVE YEARS: Lists the schools attended and the years of graduation.

FAMILY PLANNING: Lists spouses and dates of marriages and divorces of the Republican. Note: This information is quite difficult to ascertain in several instances. For some reason, Republicans don't like talking about their ex-spouses.

SELECTED ELECTION SCORECARD: Includes major campaigns for president, the U.S. Senate, the U.S. House of Representatives, and state governor. Continuous elections to the same office are indicated by the year of first election to the year of last election (i.e., 1984–90). No distinction has been made between running for the presidency in a primary (to be chosen by Republican Party delegates as the candidate) or running in the general election. Note: The terms of federal office are as follows: U.S. House of Representatives, two years; U.S. Senate, six years; president, four years.

QUICKIE BIO

A brief biography of the politician.

_____ DOES THE DUMBEST THINGS

Lists the dumbest incidents in the career of the politician

I have worked hard to provide the most accurate, up-to-date, and dumbest information available. All the anecdotes in this book have appeared previously in other publications. If you want more details, or you notice any errors, or if you know of some dumb stuff I have overlooked, please e-mail me at _politicians@dumbest.com_. Your nation (and my publisher) will thank you.

THE
REPUBLICANS

Spiro Agnew

FACTS OF LIFE

ORIGIN: Born Spiro Theodore Agnew, November 9, 1918, Baltimore, Maryland; died of leukemia, September 17, 1996, Berlin, Maryland.

FORMATIVE YEARS: University of Baltimore Law School, never received an official degree, but passed the Maryland bar in 1947.

FAMILY PLANNING: Married Elinor "Judy" Isabel Judefind, May 27, 1942.

SELECTED ELECTION SCORECARD: 1966: won, governor, Maryland (resigned 1969). 1968–72: won, vice president of U.S., under Pres. Richard M. Nixon (resigned 1973). (Only the second vice president in history to resign. The first was Andrew Jackson's vice president, John C. Calhoun, who resigned in 1832.)

QUICKIE BIO

When he was looking for a presidential running mate in 1968, Richard Nixon said that he wanted a "political eunuch." Nixon's young assistant, Pat Buchanan, recommended the best such one for the job, Spiro "Ted" Agnew. Born in Baltimore to a Greek immigrant restaurant owner, Agnew served in the army in World War II and Korea, and went to law school at night on the G. I. Bill. He got into local politics, and won election to the

15

Baltimore County Zoning Board of Appeals. Later, he served as the Baltimore County Executive, basically, the mayor of Baltimore, from 1962 to 1966. Hailed as the "New Suburban Man," Spiro changed from a Democrat to a Republican and from a liberal to a conservative after he won election as Maryland's governor. As vice president, Agnew made a name for himself as a basher of "radiclibs" (radical liberals), but his political career crashed and burned in 1973. Agnew later became buddies with entertainer Frank Sinatra, who once loaned him $250,000. In 1980, Spiro wrote a book in which he claimed his political downfall was due to the fact that he was "framed" by the Nixon administration. The title of the book? *Go Quietly . . . Or Else.*

SPIRO AGNEW DOES THE DUMBEST THINGS

★ When Nixon announced Agnew as his vice president in 1968, a reporter surveyed random private citizens on what Spiro Agnew was. Two of the answers: "Some kind of disease," and, "It's some kind of egg."

★ After riots in Baltimore in April 1968, Spiro called a meeting of moderate local black leaders. He accused them of having "a perverted concept of race loyalty," and said that they were afraid of being called "Uncle Charlie's boy" or "Uncle Tom." "Don't you think I know I'm committing political suicide when I sit here and do this?" Agnew told the leaders. "I know it." They knew it too, and most of them walked out of the meeting.

★ Following the late 1960s riots in Baltimore, Agnew criticized a police officer who refused to shoot a looter for stealing a pair of shoes. The politician claimed that sparing the shoe thief displayed the "insidious relativism that has crept into our thinking."

★ Spiro became even more bizarre during his second year as governor. He slashed health and welfare budgets, and attacked the Poor People's Campaign as "the so-called poor people—with Cadillacs."

★ "A spirit of national masochism prevails," Vice President Agnew announced to the public, "encouraged by an effete corps of impudent snobs who characterize themselves as intellectuals." Echoing the anti-intellectualism of China's revered leader Mao Tse Tung, Agnew suggested that Americans should "sweep that kind of garbage out of our society."

✪ White House staffer Pat Buchanan helped Spiro write some of his more "memorable" lines criticizing opponents of the ongoing and escalating Vietnam War. Some of Agnew's greatest bon mots: "merchants of hate," "ideological eunuchs," "parasites of passion," "supercilious sophisticates," "hopeless, hysterical hypochondriacs of history," "vicars of vacillation," "pusillanimous pussyfooting," and "nattering nabobs of negativism."

✪ Agnew was a big fan of the *Reader's Digest* monthly column "It Pays to Increase Your Word Power." In some speeches, in order to display his newly expanded vocabulary, the vice president used such erudite terms as "struthious" and "tomentose."

✪ According to reporters, when the vice president went to Kenya in 1971, his "main outing was to a nearby hunting lodge, where, in company with his private physician and his pretty, red-haired secretary, he watched two rhinos copulating."

✪ While visiting Ethiopia, Kenya, and the Congo, Spiro met such African rulers as Haile Selassie, Jomo Kenyatta, and Mobutu Sese Seko. Agnew declared, "The black leadership in the United States . . . could learn much by observing the work that has been done in these countries. . . ." Rep. William Clay (D-Missouri) reacted to Spiro's observations about some of the world's most ruthless rulers by saying, "In my opinion . . . our vice president is seriously ill. . . . His recent tirade against black leadership is just part of a game played by him—called mental masturbation."

✪ Agnew liked to play golf, but had a bad habit of whacking bystanders with his balls. White House aides called him Spiro the clown.

✪ Spiro once played tennis with the head of the Peace Corps as his doubles partner, and smashed a tennis ball into the back of the man's head. The Peace Corps executive quickly put on a motorcycle helmet for protection.

✪ At a Republican dinner in 1970, Agnew spoke out against rock music that had a pro-drug message. "We should listen more carefully to popular music, because . . . at its worst it is blatant drug-culture propaganda." To demonstrate his point Agnew quoted the lyrics from the song "Acid Queen" by the Who, which is an anti-drug song.

✪ In 1973, a federal grand jury in Maryland launched an investigation of Vice President Agnew. He was charged with fifty alleged violations of federal bribery, extortion, conspiracy, and tax laws. To a group of Republican women holding signs that read "Spiro Is Our Hero!" Agnew declared, "I will not resign if indicted! I will not resign if indicted!" On October 10, 1973, Agnew appeared in federal court, and pleaded no contest to a forty-five-page bill of charges. He resigned from the vice presidency that same day.

★ In the 1980s, Agnew became an "international consultant." One of his better paying gigs was arranging for the sale of $181 million worth of uniforms by Romanian dictator Nicolae Ceausescu to the ruler of Iraq, Saddam Hussein.

Dick Armey

FACTS OF LIFE

ORIGIN: Born Richard K. Armey, July 7, 1940, Cando, North Dakota.

FORMATIVE YEARS: Jamestown College, B.A. 1963; University of North Dakota, M.A. 1964; University of Oklahoma, Ph.D. 1969.

FAMILY PLANNING: Married Jeanine Gale (college student), 1962; divorced, 1976; married Susan Byrd Oxendine (college student), 1977.

SELECTED ELECTION SHOWCARD: 1984–98: won, U.S. House of Representatives, 26th District, Texas.

QUICKIE BIO

The man from Cando (pronounced Can Do), North Dakota, stampeded into Congress as part of the Ronald Reagan Republican herd of the 1980s, where he earned the nickname "Dr. No" for his resistance to just about everything. The man hailed as "the Republican leadership's one man brain trust" was once warned by his high school advisor not to even think about going to college. He went anyway, leaving behind his 250-pound mother, who, in his words, had "the heart of an elephant." Armey quickly became a "bush league professor at a bush league school," and taught economics at North Texas State University in Denton. When Armey tired of campus political infighting, he moved into national politics with the help of Eddie Chiles, a North Texas oil man who ran a radio campaign declaring that it was time to cut back on government waste by putting "a fence between the hogs and the trough." Eddie led Armey to the government trough, and helped him win

19

election to a newly redrawn Republican district in the suburbs of Dallas. Dick believed in the "flat tax" the way folks used to believe in the "flat earth," and proclaimed his passionate belief in the free market. Armey, the House Majority Leader who decried "The Invisible Foot of Government," spent his entire career collecting a government paycheck.

DICK ARMEY DOES
THE DUMBEST THINGS

✪ As a high school student, Armey received a D in a class called "Philosophy of Life." When he served in Congress, Dick led the Republican call for a new morality. But while teaching at North Texas State University, Armey was accused by three of his female students of alleged "inappropriate" behavior. His colleagues recalled that Dick enjoyed "bird-dogging" coeds. He divorced his first wife to marry one of his students. She cancelled the wedding three times, then finally agreed to tie the matrimonial knot. "If it were me that had documented personal conduct along the lines of the president [Clinton]," the student-loving professor later declared, "I would be so filled with shame that I would resign." It should be noted that he did not do so in his own case.

✪ In running for Congress, Dick's chief goal apparently had little to do with ideology. He realized that his over $75,000 salary as a member of Congress was a lot more attractive than his $34,000 annual income as a professor. When asked about his interest in a federal paycheck, the government-bashing economist declared, "I don't want to lose money if I decide to run." In his first campaign in 1984, Armey called for a phase out of the Social Security system. He quickly changed his position and admitted, "I didn't know what I was doing."

✪ After he was elected to Congress, thrifty Armey slept on a cot in the House gym. When House Speaker Tip O'Neill (D-Massachusetts) booted him out of the exercise facility, Dick slept on a cot in his office.

✪ When pundit William Kristol and presidential loser Steve Forbes sat on a couch in his office, Armey sighed, "There hasn't been so much brain-power assembled on that couch since I used to sleep there alone."

✪ During a House debate, Armey angrily shouted at the Democrats, "On our side, we don't care what happens to your president!" Dick later had to apologize for suggesting that Bill Clinton wasn't president of the *entire* country, and said, "You won't find me doing that again."

✪ Though praised as a "think tank in cowboy boots," Armey sometimes just didn't make sense to the average listener. When chiding a fellow member of Congress for criticizing the House Ethics Committee, Dick declared, "For him to say, 'Well, never mind you guys who are tolling in the vineyard that I committed to work in, I'm going to jump ship and go join hands with the political background noise that indicts you in total disregard of your personal commitment to a hard task,' I think is not acceptable."

★ "Hillary Clinton bothers me a lot," the former economics professor confessed to a group of real estate agents. "I realized the other day that her thoughts sound a lot like Karl Marx. She hangs around a lot of Marxists. All her friends are Marxists." Later, Armey told the First Lady, "The reports on your charm are overstated and the reports on your wit are understated."

★ When Dick Armey obtained a newswire story in 1998, he handed the item to seventy-one-year-old Rep. Bob Stump (R-Arizona) and asked him to make an announcement. "Mr. Speaker, I have the sad responsibility to tell you this afternoon that Bob Hope passed away," a solemn faced Stump declared on the floor of the House. "We will all miss him very much." When he heard the announcement, a very much alive Bob Hope laughed and said, "They were wrong, weren't they?" Armey had not noticed that the news story had been prepared in advance of Hope's death. The time and place of death were marked by XXXs. Armey later acknowledged his mistake and apologized to "Bob Hope, his family, and the entire nation."

★ After he made his famous Barney Fag faux pas, Armey blubbered, "I do not want Barney Frank to believe for one minute that I would use a slur against him. . . . I had trouble with alliteration. I was stumbling, mumbling." Armey didn't realize that "Frank" and "fag" aren't at all alliterative. Frank didn't believe the alliteration rationale either. "I rule out that it was an innocent mispronunciation," the Massachusetts Democrat observed. "I turned to my own expert, my mother, who reports that in fifty-nine years of marriage, no one ever introduced her as 'Elsie Fag.' " In 1998, a *Washington Post* photograph misidentified Armey as "Barney Frank."

Bob Barr

FACTS OF LIFE

ORIGIN: Born Robert Barr, November 5, 1948, Iowa City, Iowa.

FORMATIVE YEARS: University of Southern California, B.A. 1970; George Washington University, M.A. 1972; Georgetown University, J.D. 1977.

FAMILY PLANNING: Married and divorced once before marrying Gail Vogel (CIA analyst), then breaking up with her in 1985; married Jerilyn Ann Dobbin (volunteer), 1987. (Barr's stormy marital history was investigated by *Hustler* magazine publisher Larry Flynt.)

SELECTED ELECTION SCORECARD: 1992: lost, U.S. Senate, Georgia. 1994–98: won, U.S. House of Representatives, 7th District, Georgia.

QUICKIE BIO

Described by his mother as "a usual obnoxious" kid, Bob Barr went on to become an outspoken congressman. An army brat like his fellow Georgia Republican Newt Gingrich, Barr spent his youth traveling the world with his family and attended high school in Tehran. After earning a law degree, he worked as a CIA analyst, moved to Georgia to practice law, and became U.S. Attorney in Atlanta, where he made a name for himself prosecuting Republicans. A twice-divorced defender of family values, Bob met his match in pornographer and magazine magnate Larry Flynt, who published a series of attacks on the conservative legislator claiming that he could "teach slippery behavior to a greased weasel." In his 1998 campaign, Barr outspent his opponent 100 to 1 but only managed to slip through to office with 55 percent of the vote.

BOB BARR DOES
THE DUMBEST THINGS

⭐ While at USC in the 1960s, Barr attended two meetings of the Young Democrats. He stopped such extracurricular activity when his mother found out about it and threatened to stop funding his education.

⭐ Representative Barr has appeared to be a strong anti-abortionist. However, one of his wives claimed that he paid $300 for her to have an abortion in 1983. Bob denied that he "suggested, urged, forced or encouraged anyone to have an abortion." But he did pay for it.

⭐ According to Bob, "The flames of hedonism, the flames of narcissism, the flames of self-centered morality are licking at the very foundations of our society; the family unit." Bob knew a lot about "licking." During his unsuccessful 1992 run for the Senate, Barr licked whipped cream off the chests of two buxom beauties at a charity event.

⭐ In June 1995, Barr introduced the Defense of Marriage Act, a Congressional bill designed to outlaw same-sex marriages. However, he was not so good at defending his own marriage. His second wife Gail worked in his law offices for a time. One of her jobs was to arrange luncheon dates with Jerilyn Dobbin, whom Barr later married.

⭐ Seemingly, Barr lost interest in his second wife Gail soon after she was diagnosed with breast cancer. In a sworn affidavit, she claimed to have asked her husband to stop campaigning for the U.S. Attorney position after her surgery and chemotherapy. Gail Barr claimed, "He told me that the campaign would take my mind off my health problems."

⭐ During his divorce from Gail, Barr refused to answer questions about alleged adultery on the advice of his divorce lawyer, who claimed that Bob's answers, "could bring upon him or his family public disgrace and infamy and forfeiture of his estate."

⭐ In 1998, Bob delivered a keynote speech to a gathering of the Council of Conservative Citizens, a racist group that insisted "integration is suicide."

⭐ Barr had such a reputation for meanness that during television appearances his wife often beeped him with the message, "Smile, honey!"

⭐ Sometimes Barr seemed to bring out the worst in others as well. For example, in April 1998, Bob complained to a young airport inspection guard that he had a plane to catch. The employee swore at Barr, and told her colleague to look through his bag slowly. When the politician demanded her name, she shoved her ID in his face, and he reportedly smacked down her arms. She charged back at him as he yelled, "Nobody swears at me!" Security guards arrived on the scene and quickly escorted the young woman away.

★ Congressman Barr was an avid defender of the death penalty. However, as an attorney, he argued in court briefs that the death penalty was "cruel and unusual punishment."

★ Bob Barr started a witch-hunt against witches who practiced their religion on army bases. He wrote a letter to the commander of Fort Hood in Texas demanding that soldiers "stop this nonsense now." Bob said that allowing witches to openly practice their faith, would have an "effect on the combat readiness of your troops" and "detrimental effects on our society more broadly speaking, which has heretofore looked to our American spirit of 'for God and Country.' " Wrote the high priest of the Sacred Well Congregation of Texas, David Oringderff, himself a retired Army major, "Intellectual and spiritual bigotry is alive and well in this country."

Sonny Bono

FACTS OF LIFE

ORIGIN: Born Salvatore Bono, February 16, 1935, Detroit, Michigan; died January 5, 1998, cause of death blunt trauma to the head, suffered by skiing into a pine tree near Reno, Nevada.

FORMATIVE YEARS: Inglewood (California) High School, graduated 1952.

FAMILY PLANNING: Married Donna Rankin (waitress), 1959; divorced, 1964; married Cherilyn "Cher" Sarkisian (singer) (when their daughter was a toddler), 1971; divorced, 1975; married Susie Coehlo (model), December 31, 1981; divorced, 1984; married Mary Whitaker (waitress), February 1986.

SELECTED ELECTION SCORECARD: 1992: lost, U.S. Senate, California. 1994–98: won, U.S. House of Representatives, 49th District, California. (Bono died in office. Mary Bono, his widow, was elected to serve out the remainder of his term.)

QUICKIE BIO

Is it dumb enough?" This was the rule-of-thumb question musician Sonny Bono learned to ask from legendary record producer Phil Spector about what the public would or would not accept. When it came to Bono and politics, yeah, it was dumb enough. Born in Detroit, raised in Southern California,

Sonny made it big in the music business when he teamed up with a long-haired teenager named Cher. The duo donned fur-lined bobcat vests and Eskimo boots to wow the 1960s with hits like "I Got You, Babe," and flops like "Pammy's on a Bummer." When their recording career sagged in the 1970s, Sonny and Cher hosted popular TV variety shows, at least until their marriage broke up. Post-Cher, Sonny flopped as a solo act and an actor. Thereafter, he opened restaurants in Los Angeles and Palm Springs and became involved in politics via a fight over building restrictions. After Sonny's election to Congress in 1994, ex-wife Cher commented that her ex-husband would be right at home in the nation's capitol because politicians were "one step below used-car salesmen." And the beat goes on . . .

SONNY BONO DOES THE DUMBEST THINGS

✪ "About two years after we moved to Hawthorne [California]," Bono recalled in his autobiography, "I was offered my first glimpse of heaven: a girl's vagina."

✪ The twenty-eight-year-old Sonny roomed with seventeen-year-old Cher for months before they started having sex. "The physical part was fine," Bono shrugged, "though I wouldn't equate it with a religious experience."

✪ Bono enjoyed intimate relations with his secretary until Cher caught him in the act. Sighed Sonny, "There's nothing like having your wife catch you with your pants down to ruin an illicit romance."

✪ Sonny had plastic surgery performed on his nose "to take it from the immense down to simply large."

✪ On tour one evening, Cher asked Sonny to leave their hotel room. Why? Because a guitarist was coming up, and Cher wanted to visit with him. Sonny left the room, found the guitarist's girlfriend and had sex with her.

✪ Sonny claimed to have been the most frequent guest on the long-running TV show *Fantasy Island* (1978–84)—no special feat, since the program featured guest celebrities past their professional prime.

✪ On his last appearance on *Fantasy Island*, Sonny only had one line of dialog: "It's a nice day, Tattoo." He blew it and said on camera, "It's a nice day, Pontoon." The late Herve Villachaize, who played Tattoo, was offended and began berating Bono. Suddenly, Sonny recalled, something snapped:

"I'm standing here getting bawled out by a midget. . . . This was God's way of telling me to forget the past and move on."

⭐ "This can be a springboard," Sonny reflected after winning a seat in the U.S. House in 1994, "[But] if you're not going to go somewhere with it, I don't get the point."

⭐ During an all-night session of the House to debate a foreign aid bill, Bono walked up to a group of members of Congress and said, "I've never been up this late unless I was getting p****."

⭐ According to wife Mary, Sonny was taking up to twenty painkillers a day for chronic back and neck pain at the time he died in a skiing accident. "I am 100 percent convinced that is why he died," she told the press. "What he did showed absolute lack of judgment. That's what these pills do."

⭐ Mary Bono ran for the Congressional seat vacated by her late husband. Her opponent was Ralph Waite, the man who played Pa Walton on TV's *The Waltons* (1972–81). Mary beat Pa. Soon after her election, however, she became irritated when a reporter asked about her political views. She demanded to know why she wasn't being asked, "What kind of shoes I'm wearing and stuff like that."

"My Italian blood was on perpetual simmer," Sonny Bono confessed. "I lived for the impetuous craving for fiery romance that had once driven me to chase my cousin to Detroit." Hot-blooded Sonny was pictured here chasing First Lady Betty Ford in 1976.
(Courtesy of Gerald R. Ford Library)

Pat Buchanan

FACTS OF LIFE

ORIGIN: Born Patrick Joseph Buchanan, November 2, 1938, Washington, D.C.

FORMATIVE YEARS: Georgetown University, B.A. 1961; Columbia University, M.S. in journalism, 1962.

FAMILY PLANNING: Married Shelley Scarney (receptionist), 1971.

SELECTED ELECTION SCORECARD: 1992–96: lost, U.S. president; 2000: potential candidate of the Reform Party for U.S. president.

QUICKIE BIO

Pat Buchanan's father, whose heroes included Sen. Joseph McCarthy (R-Wisconsin), held lighted matches to his young son's hand to show him what hell was like. "See how this feels," "Pop" Buchanan, an accountant, snarled. "Now imagine that for all eternity." Many Americans felt that hell would be having Pat Buchanan as president. Buchanan billed himself as a political force, although he was never elected to any public office. The third of nine children born to a proudly Catholic family in Washington, D.C., Pat worked as a newspaper writer before joining the Nixon administration as a speechwriter and ideological bomb thrower. After Nixon fell from political grace in 1974, Buchanan made a fortune as a commentator on TV shows like *Crossfire, Capital Gang,* and *The McLaughlin Group* interspersed with gigs as a speechwriter for Presidents Gerald Ford and Ronald Reagan. The loquacious conservative became the Pat Paulsen of the far right, campaigning for president on a platform of protectionism and xenophobia that he dubbed "America First." "America First" consistently ran last with the majority of American voters, pushing Buchanan to pathetically painful political posturing. Claimed Pat, "Whatever our positions lost in logic might be recovered with invective."

PAT BUCHANAN DOES
THE DUMBEST THINGS

✪ As a boy, Buchanan threw snowballs at a bus he and his friends dubbed "Boston Blackie" because it carried inner-city maids to their jobs in Washington's affluent suburbs.

✪ Once for a joke, Pat called his family's African-American maid outside and supposedly squirted a water hose at her. Later the politician claimed, "race was never a preoccupation with us; we never thought about it."

✪ Pat was stopped for speeding and reportedly punched the arresting officer. He was suspended from Georgetown University for the assault, but finally graduated. In New York, at the Columbia School of Journalism, Buchanan ran into more trouble for reportedly fighting with a fellow student.

✪ Buchanan became a speech writer for the Nixon Administration and wrote speeches for Vice President Spiro Agnew. Poetic pen-pushing Pat prompted pedantic Agnew to label anti-Vietnam War senators "solons of sellout," "pampered prodigies," "vicars of vacillation," and "troglodytic leftists."

✪ While serving in the Nixon White House, Pat reportedly came up with the idea of using Republican Party funds to secretly finance an African-American third party that would siphon off votes from the Democrats. President Nixon's chief of staff Bob Haldeman reportedly told the president, "Buchanan . . . says that if we're going to spend $50 million in this campaign, then 10 percent of it, $5 million, ought to be devoted to financing a black." When Jesse Jackson's name came up, Nixon suggested offering Jackson $100,000 for every percentage point of the vote he won in the election.

✪ After Pat launched his 1992 presidential campaign, at a rally for him at Dartmouth College in New Hampshire, Buchanan termed a Bush campaign strategist "a geisha girl for the new world order," and mocked Jack S. Kemp, the Secretary of Housing and Urban Development, saying that he had "gone native."

Pat Buchanan (left—ooops, I mean center) was once arrested for carrying a hangman's noose onto the grounds of the Soviet Embassy in Washington and threatening to string up the Soviet ambassador.

(Courtesy of Reuters/Jim Bourg/ Archive Photos)

★ On the campaign trail, Buchanan described Congress as "Israeli occupied territory." Former Ku Klux Klan leader David Duke got angry. He claimed that Buchanan was stealing his lines.

★ During the 1992 presidential campaign, Pat denounced the government for funding abortions for Peace Corps volunteers. He characterized the policy as "shelling out fifty grand a year to execute the unborn children of upper-middle class bimbos whose idea of bringing civilization to the Third World is to take a tumble in the hay with the local witch doctor."

★ Pat had his own special take on most subjects. For example, during Ronald Reagan's presidency, he observed, "Rail as they will against 'discrimination,' women are simply not endowed by nature with the same measures of single-minded ambition and the will to succeed in the fiercely competitive world of Western capitalism." He explained further, "The momma bird builds the nest. So it was, so it ever shall be. Ronald Reagan is not responsible for this; God is."

★ Once, Pat blasted several female lobbyists, saying, "We ought to send those chicks back to the kitchen where they belong."

⭐ In 1996, Buchanan announced, "I will stop this massive illegal immigration [from Mexico] cold. Period. Paragraph. I'll build that security fence, and we'll close it, and we'll say, 'Listen Jose, you're not coming in.' " Pat later posed for reporters while sneaking through a hole in the fence along the U.S./Mexico border.

⭐ Buchanan approved of certain illegal activities. In 1986, during the height of the Iran-Contra scandal, Pat declared, "If Colonel [Oliver] North ripped off the Ayatollah and took $30 million and gave it to the Contras, then God bless Colonel North!" Pat explained further, "It is not whether some technical laws were broken, but whether we stop communism in Central America."

⭐ Buchanan hated communists much more than he detested Nazis. In 1999, Buchanan published a book, *A Republic Not an Empire*, in which he claimed that Adolf Hitler posed "no physical threat to the United States." In addition, Buchanan argued that the United States and the West might have been better off if Great Britain and France had not declared war on the Third Reich, and claimed that, after 1940, "Hitler made no overt move to threaten U.S. vital interests."

⭐ Buchanan once described Chinese leader Deng Xiaoping as an "eighty-five-year-old chain-smoking Communist dwarf."

⭐ In 1992, news analyst Michael Kinsley asked Pat Buchanan, "You've either been in the media or the government. You never had an honest job in your life and you've never run anything in your life. What makes you qualified to be president and run the whole country and makes you qualified to portray yourself as some sort of outsider populist?" Buchanan declared, "I am in Washington, not of it."

Dan Burton

FACTS OF LIFE

ORIGIN: Born Danny Lee Burton, June 21, 1938, Indiana.

FORMATIVE YEARS: Attended Indiana University in 1958 and Cincinnati Bible Seminary in 1959, but never received a degree.

FAMILY PLANNING: Married Barbara Jean Logan (secretary), 1959.

SELECTED ELECTION SCORECARD: 1978: lost, U.S. House of Representatives, 6th District, Indiana. 1982–98: won, U.S. House of Representatives, 6th District, Indiana.

QUICKIE BIO

When Hoosier politicians and pundits gathered," a longtime Indianapolis reporter recalled, "they would tell each other stories about Burton scoring with interns and pages, scoring with staffers in his offices and staffers in his campaign, scoring with Carmel [a northern suburb of Indianapolis] housewives and some fine and famous Christian women elsewhere in his district." Dan Burton grew up defending himself from his father, a violent Indiana policeman who beat his family, divorced his wife, and then kidnapped her. Danny worked his way up from the bottom, by shining shoes and caddying at a local country club. He peddled his country club polish into a fortune in the insurance business and into campaign victories in the Indiana state legislature beginning in 1966. After he finally was elected to the U.S. House of Representatives, Burton sought to position himself as a "family values" candidate. However, because of his reputation as a supposed philanderer, he

32

often was roasted with the following joke: "He [Burton] wants to become the District of Columbia's first senator. Why, you ask? Because someone told him that three-quarters of the million people in Washington go to bed each night without a senator . . ."

DAN BURTON DOES
THE DUMBEST THINGS

★ Burton, who described himself as a "pit bull" of the far right, was furious about the fact that the White House answered letters addressed to Socks, the Clintons' cat.

★ Dan believed that a conspiracy was responsible for the death of White House attorney Vince Foster on July 20, 1993. Upset when investigators ruled Foster's demise a suicide, the Indiana congressman conducted his own investigation. It included recreating Foster's death in Burton's backyard by shooting a bullet into a "headlike thing." Dan never revealed whether the "headlike thing" was a pumpkin or a watermelon.

★ During his 1988 Congressional campaign, Burton admitted to fathering an illegitimate child. The boy, who was born in 1983, was conceived during Dan's first successful run for Congress. What was Burton's campaign slogan while he was busy sewing his wild oats? "A man who cares."

★ Rebecca Hyatt began babysitting for Burton's family. According to both her former husband and a past boyfriend, big daddy Danny supposedly pressured the babysitter into having a relationship. "I've got a problem at work," the ex-boyfriend reportedly recalled Rebecca saying. "Dan wants me to have sex with him. He keeps bugging me every day." After the alleged affair started, Burton brought his former babysitter to Washington and found her a job on his Congressional staff as an "assistant to the administrative assistant."

★ As three lobbyists for Planned Parenthood were leaving Burton's office one day in the early 1990s, Dan pulled one woman back. "I was there maybe thirty seconds," she claimed, "and he had his hands up my skirt so fast I didn't even know what was coming."

★ At another time, two male lobbyists were shocked to find one of Burton's male staff members crouched under a desk taking photos up the skirt of one of Dan's female staff members. Purportedly, the man was just checking to determine whether an unscrupulous person possibly could take pictures up a woman's skirt undetected.

★ The manager of Burton's 1998 political campaign was Claudia Keller, a self-described TV "spokesmodel." Over the years, she was reportedly paid $265,479 from Burton's campaign funds, plus over $50,000 for campaign-related expenses. This included $250 a month rent for the use of her home as Burton's campaign headquarters, even though her residence was not even located in Dan's Congressional district. According to Keller's neighbors, Claudia sometimes appeared on her doorstep in a teddy to greet her favorite congressman when he arrived for one of his frequent visits.

★ Keller's compensation included fees paid to her to appear at Burton campaign events dressed as a clown.

★ Burton had very interesting political rivals. One of them was gas station attendant Bob Kern who was Dan's Democratic challenger in 1998. Reportedly, Kern had served two years in prison for theft and forgery, though he escaped conviction on charges of prostitution. When his cash card didn't work during the campaign, Kern supposedly threatened to open fire on bank employees with an Uzi. Kern allegedly impersonated a female judge over the telephone and pretended to be actress Tanya Roberts in phone calls to the media. Asked why he chose Roberts, formerly a co-lead on TV's *Charlie's Angels* during its 1980–81 season, Kern explained, "Out of all the Angels, she was my favorite." During a campaign interview on Comedy Central, the cable network, Kern claimed that he had dressed up like a woman, but denied that he was a cross dresser. "Bad press, good press—it doesn't matter to me," Kern bragged. "I'm a household name now."

★ While Burton's staff was investigating illegal contributions to the Clinton-Gore campaign by a Buddhist temple, Dan himself was forced to return two "illegal" contributions given to his campaign by temples of the Sikh religion. Burton's staff claimed that they believed the word "Gurudwara," which means temple in the Punjabi language, was a person's first name.

George Bush

All-American Presidential Bonus Chapter

DUMBEST QUOTES

"I have opinions of my own—strong opinions—but I don't always agree with them."

"High-tech is potent, precise, and in the end, unbeatable. The truth is, it reminds a lot of people of the new way I pitch horseshoes. Would you believe some of the people? Would you believe our dog? Look, I want to give the high-five symbol to high-tech."

"That I'm out of touch with the American people, that I don't know people are hurting, I know it. I feel it. We pray about it, and I mean that literally at night, and, uh, many things, the various, where I don't care about, I don't know about education or don't, I mean, we've got a sound approach, innovative, revolutionary approach, and so I have to make it that clear."

"I'm all for [bandleader/TV personality] Lawrence Welk. Lawrence Welk is a wonderful man. He used to be, or was, or—wherever he is now, bless him."

FACTS OF LIFE

ORIGIN: Born George Herbert Walker Bush, June 12, 1924, Milton, Massachusetts.

FORMATIVE YEARS: Yale University, B.A. 1948.

FAMILY PLANNING: Married Barbara Pierce (college student), January 6, 1945.

SELECTED ELECTION SCORECARD: 1962: lost, U.S. Senate, Texas. 1966–68: won, U.S. House of Representatives, 7th District, Texas. 1970: lost, U.S. Senate, Texas. 1980–84: won, U.S. vice president, under Pres. Ronald Reagan. 1988: won, U.S. president. 1992: lost, U.S. president.

QUICKIE BIO

George Bush was the golden retriever of American presidents, a gangling, good-hearted, goofy guy, who campaigned for a "kinder, gentler nation" lit by "a thousand points of light." Unfortunately for Bush, his tongue often ran well ahead of his mind, resulting in myriad points of utter confusion. Bush was a true blueblood whose father was a wealthy Wall Street banker, a U.S. senator, and president of the United States Golf Association. Bush attended the Andover prep school (team color: blue), and Yale University (team color: blue), joined the navy (team color: blue), flew fifty-eight combat missions in World War II, was shot down over the Pacific, and received the Distinguished Flying Cross for his bravery in action. After the war, he set out with his young family for the oil fields of West Texas. His bride, Barbara, claimed that George was "the first man I ever kissed" and shared the bathroom of their first Texas love nest with a mother-daughter team of prostitutes. Bush cofounded Zapata Petroleum in the 1950s, then moved to Houston, where he caught the first ripple of the Republican tsunami that eventually swept the Lone Star State. He served in the U.S. House of Representatives, and was director of the CIA in 1976–77, before entering presidential politics in 1980 and flying into office as vice president under Ronald Reagan. Not satisfied with this subordinate post, an office once described by Franklin Roosevelt's vice president, "Cactus" Jack Garner (D-Texas), as "a bucket of warm piss," Bush won the White House in 1988, overcame Iraq in a brief war, and then lost the 1992 presidential election to Bill Clinton. "I've learned the power of the word of a president," Bush philosophized. "Not maybe necessarily to make—to get something done, but the power of the word."

GEORGE BUSH DOES
THE DUMBEST THINGS

⭐ After Bush served as chief of the U.S. Liaison Office in China (1974), a reporter asked him if he had mixed with the locals. "Oh, yes," Bush enthused. "They gave us a boy to play tennis with."

★ In 1980, while campaigning for the Republican presidential nomination, Bush referred to Reagan's supply-side economic theories as "voodoo economics." After he became Reagan's vice-presidential running mate, George denied he had ever said it and challenged "anybody to find it." The NBC network immediately broadcast a video of Bush saying "voodoo economics."

★ Upon being elected vice president on the Ronald Reagan ticket in 1980, one of George's first questions was, "Well, what do we do now?"

★ Vice President Bush summed up his relationship with Pres. Ronald Reagan by saying, "There's no difference between me and the president on taxes. No more nit-picking. Zip-a-dee-doo-dah. Now it's off to the races."

★ When asked in 1984 why he switched from being pro-choice to being anti-abortion, George declared, "There are an awful lot of things I don't remember."

★ Environmentalist Vice President Bush on the threat to caribou from the Alaska pipeline: "Caribou like the pipeline. They lean up against it, have a lot of babies, scratch on it. There's more damn caribou than you can shake a stick at."

★ While touring the Nazi concentration camps at Auschwitz in September 1987, Vice President Bush looked around and commented, "Boy, they were big on crematoriums, weren't they?"

★ In August 1986, George visited the Middle East and queried a top ranking Jordanian official, "Tell me, General, how dead is the Dead Sea?" The official answered, "Very dead, sir."

★ When asked in 1988 if his Vice President George Bush had had any impact on White House decisions, Ronald Reagan commented, "I can't answer in that context."

★ At a campaign appearance in Idaho during the 1988 presidential race, Bush thought back to the eight years he served as vice president under Ronald Reagan and commented, "We have had triumphs, we have had made mistakes, we have had sex."

★ In March 1992, Reagan told the press his opinion of George Bush, "He doesn't seem to stand for anything." Later when Reagan refused to appear at a fundraiser for Bush, George's White House explained that "Reagan was too senile to make an appearance."

★ In January 1987, Bush spoke with typical eloquence about the Iran-Contra scandal, in which the Reagan administration was involved in selling arms to Iran and sending money to revolutionaries in Nicaragua. "On the surface," the vice president observed, "selling arms to a country that sponsors terrorism, of course, clearly, you'd have to argue it's wrong, but it's the exception sometimes that proves the rule."

★ In January 1988, veteran TV newsman Dan Rather confronted Bush about his role in the Iran-Contra affair. George snapped, "It's not fair to judge my whole career by a rehash of Iran. How would you like it if I judged your career by those seven minutes when you walked off the set in New York?" Rather had indeed walked off the air in Miami, but shouted back, "Mr. Vice President, you've made us hypocrites in the face of the world! How could you?"

★ Later on the TV show *Nightline*, Bush repeatedly referred to host Ted Koppel as "Dan." When Ted told Bush, "Dan [Rather]'s the other fellow," Bush responded, "It's Freudian, hey, listen, it's Freudian. I promise you, it's Freudian." When he called Ted Dan again, George's media consultant taped a sign below the camera that read, TED.

★ On the election trail in May 1988, George visited a drug rehab center and asked a patient, "What did you start out on, just for the heck of it?" Later he asked another patient, "Did you go through a withdrawal thing?"

★ At a campaign rally in October 1988, Bush made this startling political analysis: "It's no exaggeration to say the undecideds could go one way or the other."

★ President Bush wondered publicly about a lot of things including: "the post-Vietnam thing," "the roots thing," "the drought thing," "the vision thing," "the gender thing," "the actual deployment thing," "the religion thing," "the civil disobedience thing," "the feminist thing," "the tarnished-image thing," "the women thing," and "the stomach thing."

★ In his 1988 speech to accept the Republican presidential nomination, Bush pronounced, "The Congress will push me to raise taxes, and I'll say no, and they'll push and I'll say no, and they'll push again. And all I can say to them is, 'Read my lips: No new taxes.' " In 1990, President Bush passed a tax increase of $137 billion, the largest in American history. At a press conference, the president explained, "Let me be clear, I'm not in favor of new taxes. I'll repeat that over and over again. And this one compromise that—where we begrudgingly have to accept revenue, revenue increases, is the exception that proves the rule . . . The rule that I'm strongly opposed to raising taxes."

"When I need a little advice about Saddam Hussein, I turn to country music," confessed President George Bush in 1991. In 1982, Vice President George Bush (left) got a little advice from soul brother #1, James Brown (center), and Rev. Al Sharpton.
(Courtesy of George Bush Presidential Library)

⭐ While planning his first presidential speech to the nation in 1989, Bush wanted a dramatic prop. His advisors reportedly suggested a bag of crack. George approved of the prop enthusiastically. The advisors wanted to have the bag of crack purchased near the White House, but unfortunately, nobody sold crack near the president's abode. So undercover DEA agents called a suspected drug dealer and asked him to deliver crack to a park near the White House. The dealer's response: "Where the f*** is the White House?" Upon clarification, the seller said, "Oh, you mean where Reagan lives." The dealer found the White House, and sold the undercover agents three ounces of crack for $2,400. Bush displayed the drugs on camera and declared, "This is crack cocaine seized a few days ago across the street from the White House."

⭐ When a high school student asked President Bush in February 1990 about whether his administration obtained ideas on education from other countries, George observed, "Well, I'm going to kick that one right into the end zone of the secretary of education. But, yes, we have all— he travels a good deal, goes abroad. We have a lot of people in the department that does that. We're having an international—this is not as much education as dealing with the environment—a big international conference coming up. And we get it all the time—exchange of ideas."

⭐ After a visit to a Maryland Head Start Center, an excited George Bush declared, "I learned an awful lot about bathtub toys—about how to work the telephone. One guy knows—several of them know their own phone numbers—preparation to go to the dentist. A lot of things I'd forgotten. So it's been a good day."

⭐ Campaigning in New Hampshire in 1992 for reelection as president, Bush lashed out at "mournful pundits," "smart-aleck columnists," "egghead academicians," and "jacklegs jumping up demanding equal time with some screwy scheme." He added, "I am sick and tired every night of hearing one of these carping little liberal Democrats jumping all over my you-know-what."

⭐ In 1992, George traveled to Japan. At a state dinner, he became violently ill and threw up on the feet of the Japanese Prime Minister Kiichi Miyazawa.

⭐ After the widely reported incident, the Japanese press coined a new word: *bushuru*. One Japanese entertainer trained a monkey to react to the command, "bushuru," by pretending to throw up on his feet.

⭐ For Bush, the episode had religious ramifications. "Somebody said . . . we prayed for you over there. That was not just because I threw up on the Prime Minister of Japan either. Where was He when I needed him? But I said, let me tell you something. . . . You cannot be president of the United States if you don't have faith. Remember Lincoln, going to his knees in times of trial in the Civil War and all that stuff. You can't be. And we are blessed. . . . So don't feel sorry for me—don't cry for me Argentina."

⭐ Bush passed a note to his vice president, Dan Quayle, in the White House. The note read, "How do you titillate an ocelot? You oscillate her tit a lot!"

⭐ In 1989 President Bush visited a class of ten- and eleven-year-olds in Chicago. He didn't know what to say until he spotted a pet rabbit in the classroom. "See that rabbit over there? Don't let him out if Millie [the Bush family pet dog] comes to this school, okay? The other day . . . running through the woods, Millie caught something and Mrs. Bush said to the Secret Service man, 'What is that?' And the Secret Service guy said, 'A bunny.' She had caught this bunny." The kids were horrified.

⭐ Looking back on his political experience, Bush observed in the late 1990s, "It has been said by some cynic, maybe it was a former president, 'If you want a friend in Washington, get a dog.' Well, we took them literally—that advice, as you know. But I didn't need that because I have Barbara Bush."

George W. Bush

FACTS OF LIFE

ORIGIN: Born George Walker Bush, July 6, 1946, New Haven, Connecticut.

FORMATIVE YEARS: Yale University, B.A. 1968; Harvard Business School, M.B.A. 1975.

FAMILY PLANNING: Married Laura Welch (librarian), November 1977.

SELECTED ELECTION SCORECARD: 1978: lost, U.S. House of Representatives, 19th District, Texas. 1994–98: won, governor, Texas. 2000: potential candidate for U.S. president.

QUICKIE BIO

According to one family friend, "The whole key to understanding George W. is his relationship with his father." Kind of like Bart and Homer Simpson. George W. (sometimes known simply as "W.") was a righteous member of the American political junior league, though he wasn't technically a junior. The eldest of five surviving children of former Pres. George Bush, the boy grew up in West Texas where he was known as "Boosto" or "the Bombastic Bushkin." He went back East to party (and study) at Phillips Academy, Andover, Yale University, and Harvard, and returned to Texas to party (and work) in the oil business. Through good luck and good connections, George survived the oil bust in the mid 1980s, became a born-again Christian, helped out with his father's presidential campaign, and managed to snag a chunk of the Texas Rangers baseball team. The Rangers started winning, and so did W., defeating bouffant-hairstyled Democrat Ann Richards for the Texas governor's office in 1994. With a huge war chest, George W. entered the race for the year 2000 presidential election. Billing himself as a "compassionate conservative," George W. closely resembled his major Democratic opponent, Vice President Albert Gore Jr. (D-Tennessee). Both Bush and Gore had political dads. They both had political granddads. They both went to Harvard. They both could have been described as "guys who were born on third base and thought they got a triple." And they were both motivated by a single passionate desire: To make Dad proud. At least George W. was not as dumb as his brother Jeb.

GEORGE W. BUSH DOES
THE DUMBEST THINGS

✪ Bush was in high school and college in the 1960s, but was completely out of touch with the contemporary political scene. About the Vietnam era, Bush recalled, "I don't remember any kind of heaviness."

✪ While at Harvard Business School in the mid 1970s, George W. reacted to the Watergate debacle by "withdrawing."

✪ Bush said his favorite musician of the 1960s was the country legend (and legendary drinker) George Jones. "I liked some of the Beatles— though the Beatles went through a weird psychedelic period which I didn't particularly care for."

✪ At college, George W. became a member of the Delta Kappa Epsilon fraternity, also known as the Dekes. When stories circulated that the fraternity branded their initiates, Bush explained that it was "only a cigarette burn."

✪ During his 1978 Congressional campaign, Bush and his staff thought it would be a good idea to offer free beer at a rally at Texas Tech University in Lubbock. The opposition distributed a letter saying, "Mr. Bush has used some of his vast sums of money . . . to persuade young college students to vote for and support him by offering free alcohol to them." Bush lost the election, and later gave up drinking.

✪ On a 1990 dove-hunting trip with photographers to prove his gun-loving Texas roots, gubernatorial candidate George W. heard his friends yell, "Shoot! Shoot!" So he shot. But instead of killing a dove, Bush blasted a killdeer, a bird that was on the protected species list. "Even when I picked the bird up off the ground I thought it was a dove," explained Bush, who had to pay a $130 fine. "They look a lot alike."

✪ Bush once argued with his mother that only Christians, not Jews nor Muslims, could get into Heaven. Barbara Bush phoned the Reverend

Billy Graham to settle the dispute. Graham answered, "I happen to agree with what George says about the interpretation of the New Testament, but I want to remind both of you to never play God." George W. later soft-pedaled the incident and claimed that he did not control who got into heaven.

★ Bush signed a Texas law in 1997 making it legal to carry licensed weapons into churches. Two years later a gunman carried a firearm into a house of worship in Fort Worth, Texas, and shot seven other people and then himself. Bush blamed the crime on "a wave of evil" and suggested that Americans "collectively pray for love in people's hearts."

★ In 1997, Bush met with Texas Democratic leader Bob Bullock over breakfast. The two discussed a bill that was soon coming up in the Texas legislature. "I'm sorry, Governor," Bullock explained, "I'm gonna have to f*** you on this one." Reportedly, George W. stood up, grabbed Bullock, pulled him forward, kissed him, and said, "If you're going to f*** me, you'll have to kiss me first."

★ On the campaign trail in 1999, Bush complained about rumors that he was photographed dancing nude on a table. "People are spreading this garbage. . . ," he grumbled. "They've lost their f***ing minds." When asked who had lost their minds, George W. answered, "Everyone who's running for president."

★ At a fundraising function in Austin, Texas, presidential candidate Bush addressed a crowd of business owners and urged Texas teenagers to "abstain from sex until you find the partner you want to marry." "Abstinence?" some women in the room laughed, "Good luck!" When W. continued to argue in favor of abstinence, one woman challenged, "Well, were you a virgin when you got married?" Bush replied, "No."

★ George W. was a whole lot smarter than his kid brothers Neil and John Ellis, the latter also known as "Jeb." Neil got caught up in the scandal surrounding the billion dollar bailout of the Silverado Banking, Savings & Loan Association in Colorado, while Jeb became a wheeler dealer in Miami, Florida. One of Jeb's best deals was working for entrepreneur Miguel Recarey in the mid 1980s, when his father was Ronald Reagan's vice president. Recarey, who reportedly carried a pistol under his jacket, hired Bush as a "real estate consultant." However, Jeb spent much of his time lobbying in Washington on behalf of Recarey's health maintenance organization. Recarey was accused of allegedly defrauding Medicare of millions of dollars, and departed for Venezuela, while Jeb won election as governor of Florida in 1998.

"I want the folks to see me sitting in the same kind of seat they sit in, eating the same popcorn, peeing in the same urinal," declared George W. Bush when he was the managing partner of the Texas Rangers baseball team.
(Courtesy of Reuters/G. Reed Schumann/Archive Photos)

⭐ Returning from a five-day trip to Paris, First Lady of Florida Columba Bush, Jeb's wife, went through customs but "forgot" to declare $19,000 worth of goods she had purchased during her visit. How did the customs agents discover the undeclared goods? Columba had left the receipts in her passport.

⭐ During his first race for governor, George W. was asked if he'd ever used illegal drugs and replied, "Maybe I did, maybe I didn't. What's the difference?" During his presidential campaign, Bush often repeated the line, "When I was young and irresponsible, I was really young and irresponsible." At one point, Bush was arrested for drunken driving, and cocaine was rumored to have been involved. Cocaine or no, Bush was ordered by a judge to perform community service.

⭐ During his campaign in 1994 against Gov. Ann Richards, bumper stickers appeared that read, ANN CAN LICK BUSH. For the 2000 presidential campaign, the anti-Bush bumper sticker was shortened to LICK BUSH.

★ When he learned of his dad's plans to celebrate his seventy-fifth birthday by parachuting out of a plane, George W. observed, "I agree with my mother's assessment when they named the Central Intelligence Agency building after him. She said, 'I can't believe they'd be naming any facility with the word intelligence in it after George Bush.' "

★ On the campaign trail in New Hampshire, Bush visited a school that was celebrating "Perseverance Month." The theme confused Bush. "This is Preservation Month," the candidate told the school children. "I appreciate preservation. This is what you do when you run for president. You've got to preserve."

★ Gov. George W. Bush didn't think it was funny when he looked at the parody Web site www.gwbush.com. Bush's staff filed a legal claim against the comedy Web page and began buying up Bush-oriented domain names, including www.bushsucks.com. Reflecting on the free press and the Internet, the governor declared, "There ought to be limits to freedom."

★ Looking forward to the 2000 presidential election, George W. declared, "If it comes down to Smart Al [Gore] versus Dumb George, I can live with that."

Helen Chenoweth-Hage

FACTS OF LIFE

ORIGIN: Born Helen Palmer, January 27, 1938, Topeka, Kansas.

FORMATIVE YEARS: Whitworth College, attended 1955–58.

FAMILY PLANNING: Married Nicholas Signor Chenoweth (lawyer), 1964; divorced, 1975; married Wayne Hage (rancher), October 2, 1999.

SELECTED ELECTION SCORECARD: 1994–98: won, U.S. House of Representatives, 1st District, Idaho.

QUICKIE BIO

Earth First!" read the front of a Helen Chenoweth T-shirt. The back read, "We'll log the other planets later." The pin-up girl for the militia movement, Helen Chenoweth was considered by many to be "dumb as a mud fence." Born in Kansas, Chenoweth moved to Idaho in 1964, presumably with her first husband. She worked as a medical and legal management consultant, then divorced and got into politics. She worked under a number of well-known Republicans before founding Consulting Associates with a partner who managed to dip his pen in the company ink. The 1980s found the little old lady from Orofino (as Chenoweth was fondly called by her supporters— Orofino is her present hometown in Idaho) involved with the sagebrush

46

rebellion, the Wise Use movement, and lobbying on behalf of industry. By the time of her election to the U.S. House, Chenoweth had become the den mother of the "county supremacy" movement, a rigidly conservative Republican whose legislative agenda included restricting U.S. citizenship to persons born here, and requiring federal agents to get the approval of county sheriffs before taking any action. And what did her opponents think of the right-wing granny? They sported bumper stickers that read, CAN HELEN, NOT SALMON.

HELEN CHENOWETH DOES
THE DUMBEST THINGS

✪ Like the conspiracy-loving militia men, Chenoweth believed that the Pentagon had a fleet of "stealth helicopters," also known as "black helicopters," poised to swoop out of the sky and take control after the federal government declared martial law. To prove her conspiracy theory, Helen declared, "I can show you a picture of a 'black helicopter.' "

✪ Helen vehemently denied that she ever attended a meeting of any militia group. But she did not deny that the Militia of Montana marketed a video presentation that she made for their members entitled *Crisis in America*.

✪ In April 1995, after the federal building in Oklahoma City was bombed, killing more than 180 people, Chenoweth condemned the federal government, not the militia-inspired bombers. "We must begin to look at the public policies that may be pushing people too far," she informed the media. "I'm not willing to condemn militias."

✪ During her 1994 campaign, Helen held "endangered salmon bake" fundraisers. A particular favorite was the sockeye salmon, whose population had been decimated in Idaho by the building of numerous dams. For a time, Chenoweth worked as a lobbyist for the hydroelectric industry.

✪ When wildlife officials announced a plan to reintroduce the grizzly bear into her state, Chenoweth fumed, "They are schizophrenic, manic-depressive animals. I don't want them at all in Idaho."

✪ Helen the politician declared that in one Idaho county, federal wildlife experts were trying to "introduce the grizzly bear without a shred of scientific evidence that the grizzly bear ever lived there. Ever." Oops! In the early nineteenth century, Lewis and Clark wrote about seeing grizzly bears in the county, and hunting and trapping records from the 1890s and 1900s reported twenty-five to forty grizzlies killed annually in the same county.

✪ After Chenoweth was elected to Congress, *The Truth at Last*, a white supremacist newspaper, claimed that her victory proved "that a race-based campaign is a WINNER."

✪ Helen opposed the U.S. Forest Service's plan to recruit minorities to work in Idaho. "The warm climate community just hasn't found the colder climate that attractive," cold-blooded Chenoweth whined. "It's an area of America that has simply never attracted the Afro-American or the Hispanic."

✪ Chenoweth campaigned on an anti-immigrant platform. However, when a Hungarian immigrant in Pennsylvania was arrested for breaking national clean-water regulations and called a federal judge "a bunch of jokers," Helen praised him as "a man who loved this country."

✪ When Chenoweth arrived in Washington, she declared that "congress-woman" was too politically correct for her. She demanded that everyone refer to her as "congressman."

✪ During the 1996 Republican primary, Bill Levinger, Chenoweth's opponent, appeared on a Boise, Idaho, television station and declared that he decided to run against Helen because he couldn't swim to Hawaii. He then explained that he had been "trying to get punched out" during the previous weekend, pulled out a wad of bills, offered a reporter $500 for a kiss, and stripped down to his socks and underwear. When Levinger refused to leave the TV station, the police were called into action. Despite the fact that Levinger reportedly spent half the campaign at a mental health unit, he still managed to attract one third of the Republican vote.

✪ Chenoweth attacked her opponent in her first Congressional race for having an adulterous relationship. During her 1998 campaign, she produced attack ads demanding that her Democratic opponent denounce Clinton's adulterous relationship with Monica Lewinsky. But late in the campaign, newspapers revealed that, allegedly, Chenoweth herself had been involved in a six-year long relationship with her married business partner, Vernon Ravenscroft. Commenting on Helen's attack ads, Ravenscroft's wife said, "I don't see how Helen can live with herself and do this."

✪ Chenoweth claimed that the difference in her affair and Clinton's was that she had never lied about hers. Oops! She had. To a reporter who produced notes made in 1995 recording her denial when she was asked point blank about the truth of her having had an adulterous relationship. "That is so bizarre," Helen told the journalist. "People who know me know better than that."

Jon Christensen

FACTS OF LIFE

ORIGIN: Born Jon Lynn Christensen, February 2, 1963, St. Paul, Nebraska.

FORMATIVE YEARS: Midland Lutheran College, B.S. 1985; South Texas College of Law, J.D. 1989.

FAMILY PLANNING: Married Meredith Stewart Maxfield (co-ed), 1987; divorced, 1995; engaged to Tara Dawn Holland (former Miss America), 1998.

SELECTED ELECTION SCORECARD: 1992: lost, U.S. House of Representatives, 2nd District, Nebraska. 1994–96: won, U.S. House of Representatives, 2nd District, Nebraska.

QUICKIE BIO

Heralded by some detractors as "the dumbest man to serve in the 104th Congress," Jon Christensen grew up in rural Nebraska, and attended college on a basketball scholarship. He never really did well on the court, but he did manage to operate an Amway distributorship out of his dorm room. Christensen tried unsuccessfully to become a lawyer. So he did what any red-blooded American would do—he sold insurance and fertilizer, and migrated into politics. Jon defeated Rep. Peter Hoagland (D-Nebraska), and traveled to

Washington to represent metropolitan Omaha in the U.S. House of Representatives. Unfortunately, Christensen never seemed to figure out how the legislative process worked and lost the 1998 Congressional elections. However, Jon did acquire money the old-fashioned way. He married it.

JON CHRISTENSEN DOES
THE DUMBEST THINGS

★ Christensen set up an organic lawn fertilizer company called "Old McDonald's," which used the phone number 1-800-EE-I-EE-I-O. Jon ran the struggling company out of his garage, but listed his title on his resume as "fertilizer holding company executive."

★ In 1994, Christensen ran for Congress against the Democratic incumbent, Peter Hoagland. During the campaign, Jon's supporters made death threats against a family that appeared in a Hoagland commercial.

★ On the radio in Nebraska, Christensen said that he believed in cutting all government "hand-outs and subsidies" to "eliminate people's reliance on government." However, when the interview pointed out that Jon himself had more than $30,000 in outstanding government student loans, the hard-driving conservative whined, "Well, I wouldn't have been able to go to school if I didn't have a student loan."

★ While running for Congress in 1994, Christensen failed to vote in a local Omaha election. He reasoned, "My life is scheduled from six in the morning till midnight, and I run off a piece of paper every moment, and I'm not, uh, not laying blame anywhere, but unfortunately I didn't have, uh, anything on that piece of paper that said, 'Vote today.' "

★ During an appearance at an Omaha high school, Christensen's campaign staff was terrified that their candidate might have to respond to questions that he had not rehearsed. So they reportedly filled the hall with students who were campaign volunteers and gave them prepared questions. The student volunteers were instructed to hold pens in their raised hands so that Christensen would know who to call on. However, word got out about the scheme, and everyone with a question held a pen in their raised hand.

★ Jon called a press conference to announce his personal plan to reduce the federal deficit. His recommendation was to cut government spending by $1.5 trillion. When a reporter informed the congressman that $1.5 trillion was the size of the entire budget, he quickly changed topics.

- Christensen's wife Meredith was from a wealthy Dallas family. Many observers claimed she had acquired a seat in Congress for her husband. After the election, at an Omaha Press Club Dinner, Meredith reportedly sang the following words to the tune of "I Will Follow Him": "He'll always have my money, my money, my money . . . as long as I'm his honey, his honey, his honey . . ."

- She wasn't his honey for long. Meredith Christensen became friendly with one of Jon's fellow first-term Republican revolutionaries, Rep. John Shadegg (R-Arizona). Shadegg was a conservative who believed in family values. Shadegg valued Christensen's family so much that he was caught reportedly "in mid-yelp" with Meredith. According to a published account, "Christensen punched Shadegg and a fistfight ensued in front of the wife, who was naked throughout the fisticuffs."

- The Christensens filed for divorce—for the third time. This time they followed through with it. Included in the divorce papers was a signed affidavit from Meredith asserting, "I regret the fact that during our marriage I have engaged in marital infidelity," and, "I was unable to remain faithful."

- On December 5, 1995, somebody claiming to be "the freshman Republican congressman from Nebraska" phoned the White House to make sure that the Secret Service would not allow Meredith Christensen into the annual White House Christmas ball the next day. Two years later, Christensen attended that White House Christmas ball with former Miss America, Tara Dawn Holland. After receiving special security clearance, Christensen proposed to Miss Holland on the south portico of the White House with the proverbs, "A virtuous woman is a crown to her husband," and, "Who can find a virtuous woman? For her price is far above rubies." People at the party knocked on the windows to distract him.

- Before making his proposal, Christensen had Tara Dawn swear to him that she was a virgin.

- Emboldened by his virgin fiancée, Christensen gave up his house seat in early 1998 and announced that he would run for governor of Nebraska. Unfortunately, he forgot to tell Nebraska's Republican Party officials about his political plans. Jon lost the election.

Tom DeLay

FACTS OF LIFE

ORIGIN: Born Thomas Dale DeLay, Laredo, Texas, April 8, 1947.

FORMATIVE YEARS: University of Houston, B.S. 1970.

FAMILY PLANNING: Married Christine Ann Furrh (high school sweetheart), 1967.

SELECTED ELECTION SCORECARD: 1984–98: won, U.S. House of Representatives, 22nd District, Texas.

QUICKIE BIO

Tom DeLay got into politics because government wouldn't let him use his favorite "poisons" to kill bugs. The son of a deeply religious oil man, young DeLay grew up in Venezuela, earned a degree in biology, and went into the pest control business. Tom became the self-described "best weasel killer in Houston," but got so fed up with bureaucratic red tape that he decided to work for the government. He won election to the Texas State House of Representatives in 1978, and was swept into the U.S. House of Representatives from the Houston area with the 1984 Republican landslide. In Washington, Tom became known as "the Exterminator" and "the Hammer" for his take-no-prisoners political style. A staunch conservative who opposed birth control, the theory of evolution, and day care, DeLay formed his own political action committee, Americans for a Republican Majority. He funneled millions of dollars to conservative candidates, while ferociously fighting campaign finance reform. Appointed Majority Whip of the House in 1995, the back-slapping, snuff-dipping DeLay liked to pose for photographers holding a whip. "I was a real jerk when I got elected," he declared. Whip it, Tom. Whip it good.

TOM DELAY DOES
THE DUMBEST THINGS

✪ DeLay named his exterminating company Albo Pest Control. He claimed that he "hated the name" but kept it because "it reminded consumers of a well-known brand of dog food."

✪ A self-proclaimed devout Christian, DeLay confessed, "I've never been able to understand that turn-the-other-cheek stuff."

✪ When Republicans were considering Dan Quayle for vice president at the 1988 national convention, Quayle's opponents claimed that he had used family connections to avoid fighting in Vietnam. DeLay, who also had not served in Vietnam, held a press conference to explain the situation. Tom's explanation? So many African-Americans had enlisted to fight the war in Vietnam that there was no room left for whites like Quayle.

✪ Conservative Christian DeLay believed in family values, or at least that certain members of his family were valuable. Tom didn't talk much to his widowed mother, and shunned a brother whom he described as "a real skid row type."

✪ In 1995, DeLay created the ultimate do-nothing Congress when he and his allies refused to reach a compromise on the U.S. budget and caused the federal government to temporarily shut its doors. Although the political posturing cost taxpayers a lot of money, Tom bragged, "Our biggest mistake was backing off from the government shut-down."

✪ At the same time he was negotiating a raise for himself and other members of Congress, Tom declared, "Working families trying to get by on $4.25 an hour don't really exist."

✪ DeLay labeled the Environmental Protection Agency the "gestapo of government pure and simple."

✪ DeLay, who sits on the House Science Committee, contended that there was no such thing as acid rain. He also said that the bald eagle was never close to extinction. During testimony about global warming, Tom declared that he had never heard of a landmark study of the issue. "It's the arrogance of man to think that man can change the climate of the world," the former exterminator proclaimed. "Only nature can change the climate, a volcano, for instance."

✪ When the Nobel committee honored researchers investigating ozone depletion in 1995, DeLay called their award "the Nobel appeasement prize," and characterized the committee as "Swedish environmental extremists." Tom also challenged the idea that chlorofluorcarbons, or CFCs, caused ozone depletion. He called the hypothesis "the Chicken Little theory."

⭐ In April 1997, Tom went ballistic during a debate on the house floor and reportedly started yelling "gutless chickens***" at Rep. David Obey (D-Wisconsin). After he pushed Obey, swore at him, and was led away by house staff, DeLay explained that the whole thing was actually Obey's fault. Tom claimed that Obey "physically provoked" him with "an invasion of personal space" by pointing at his chest during a debate. Obey told DeLay, "Grow up."

⭐ In July 1998, Russell Eugene Weston burst into DeLay's office, fired a .38 caliber pistol, and killed John Gibson, DeLay's bodyguard, before being apprehended. It was rumored that Weston was part of a conspiracy to assassinate the entire Republican leadership of the House. Actually, Weston was a lone gunman with a reported history of mental illness. In 1996, he had visited the CIA, and claimed that he was a clone and the son of John F. Kennedy. DeLay's spokesman told the press, "Some people say if more people had guns, we could have defended ourselves better against this kind of crazy gunman."

⭐ Various rumors about affairs have surrounded DeLay's personal life. Tom has denied all the gossip, but commented, nonetheless, in 1998, "This town [Washington] is full of rumors. Unfortunately, most of the time, the rumors are true."

"I bought me a truck, started killing bugs. That's all I knew, how to make money..." explained Tom DeLay (center), pointing out an unidentified critter to Newt Gingrich (left) and Dick Armey (right).
(Courtesy of Reuters/Ira Schwarz/ Archive Photos)

Bob Dole

FACTS OF LIFE

ORIGIN: Born Robert Joseph Dole, July 22, 1923, Russell, Kansas.

FORMATIVE YEARS: Kansas University, attended 1941–43; University of Arizona, attended 1948–49; Washburn Municipal University, B.B., LL.B. 1952.

FAMILY PLANNING: Married Phyllis Holden (occupational therapist), June 12, 1948; divorced, 1972; married Elizabeth "Liddy" Hanford (lawyer/bureaucrat), December 6, 1975.

SELECTED ELECTION SCORECARD: 1960–68: won, U.S. House of Representatives, 1st District, Kansas. 1968–96: won, U.S. Senate, Kansas. 1976: lost, vice president, running with presidential candidate Gerald Ford. 1996: lost, U.S. president.

QUICKIE BIO

In the 1950s, Bob Dole joked that he had "suffered some head injury in the war and then had gone into politics." Maybe that's what turned a Kansas country boy into one of America's most abrasive, impatient, and quirky politicians. Those close to him often talked about two Bob Doles—"Bad Bob" and "Good Bob." "Good Bob" left Kansas to serve as an army infantryman in World War II, was wounded in Italy, and was left for dead. He eventually recovered, though he lost the use of his right arm. Back in Kansas, he jumped into politics and won election to the state legislature in 1950, while he was still studying for his law degree. He then served as a county attorney until 1960 when he successfully ran for U.S. House of Representatives and held public office in Washington, D.C., for the next forty years. "Bad Bob" didn't help raise his daughter, left his first wife, and made so many controversial comments that he consistently lost national elections. Dole's ambitious second wife, Liddy, was born to a wealthy North Carolina family, attended Duke, Harvard Law School, and Oxford, and worked for Presidents Johnson, Nixon, and Reagan. She was appointed the Secretary of Transportation in 1983, the Secretary of Labor in 1989, then two years later became president of the American Red Cross—definitely one of the most powerful secretaries in American history. At various times in his career, Pa Dole was known as "Senator Flip-flop," "Senator Straddle," and "Senator Gridlock," but never President Dole. Looking back on his efforts to win the presidency, Bob sighed, "I went for the jugular—my own."

BOB DOLE DOES
THE DUMBEST THINGS

✪ When asked which one of his personal qualities voters wanted to know about, Dole responded, "Beats me."

✪ Both Republicans and Democrats recruited Bob to run for office after World War II. Why? According to Dole, "They thought I'd get elected because I'd been shot." Dole became a Republican because there were more Republicans than Democrats in his district.

✪ For his first 1960 Congressional race, Bob enlisted twenty pretty young women dressed in identical red felt skirts and matching handbags, accompanied by a woman playing a ukulele and a quartet of female singers called the "Bobolinks." His opponent lost and declared, "You drowned me in pineapple juice." Dole campaigned with the Bobolinks, later christened "Dolls for Dole" until his 1974 Senate campaign.

✪ In Dole's 1964 Congressional campaign against Bill Bork, Bob appeared in radio and television commercials to recite a simple message: "Bork is a jerk."

✪ Dole married Phyllis Holden, a physical therapist who was instrumental in helping him overcome his wartime injuries. They had a daughter, about whom Bob said, "I don't think I really knew her very well." Daddy Dole's excuse? He was "married to politics."

✪ He may have been wed to politics, but Dole reportedly did have time to have an outside romance during the last four years of his first marriage. The press learned of the purported relationship during Dole's 1996 election campaign, but he managed to keep it out of the papers. When asked whether he was in love with second wife Liddy, the senator grumbled, "Love is a disease of youth."

✪ When young Liddy told her mother she was going to Harvard Law School, her parent walked into the bathroom and barfed.

After Bob Dole fell off the stage at a 1996 presidential campaign rally in California, his staffers had the band play the Elton John tune "I'm Still Standing" at Dole rallies. When the staffers realized that the song included the lyric "You'll wind up like the wreck you hide behind the mask you use," they stopped playing the song.
(Courtesy of Reuters/Rick T. Wilkins/Archive Photos)

⭐ After getting a job with the White House Office of Consumer Affairs in 1968, Liddy marched into the White House and announced to President Johnson's staff, "I come with a slot!"

⭐ A date once invited Liddy Dole to a Washington Redskins football game. She showed up with her briefcase, and spent the entire game reading documents. Her escort was not happy. "I said I would go to the game," Liddy explained. "I didn't say I would watch it."

⭐ "Bad Bob" Dole had a nasty tongue. Dole on Democratic presidential candidate Michael Dukakis: "Dukakis? Never had it." Dole on George H. W. Bush: "He screws with his socks on." Dole on Dan Quayle: "Mr. Potato Head." Dole on Ronald Reagan: "A befuddled septuagenarian." When diminutive Sen. Howard Baker (R-Tennessee) dropped out of the 1980 Republican presidential primary, Bob snipped, "Howard can now open a tall men's shop in Japan." He dubbed Presidents Ford, Carter, and Nixon, "See No Evil, Hear No Evil, and Evil."

⭐ "A lot of people think I'm grumpy," "Good Bob" observed, "but you have to remember, my wife's president of the Red Cross. I never know how much blood I gave during the night."

⭐ Dole campaigned as vice president in 1976 on a ticket with Pres. Gerald Ford. Many complained that Dole's abrasive political style lost the Republicans the election that year. Bob called Democratic presidential candidate Jimmy Carter a "hypocrite," and asked, "Would you buy a used peanut from Jimmy Carter?" When asked why he needed to be so vicious, Dole replied, "You want to leave a little raw meat in the audience."

- Debating Democratic vice presidential candidate Walter Mondale during the 1976 election, Dole observed, "If we added up all the killed and wounded in Democrat wars in this century it would be about 1.6 million Americans, enough to fill the city of Detroit." Shortly after, the Ford-Dole ticket sank in the polls and they lost the election.

- Dole's presidential ambitions did not die in 1976, though his international reputation did. In April 1990, Bob met with Pres. Saddam Hussein of Iraq, who had vowed to turn Israel into a "sea of fire." Two days after conferring with Saddam, Dole met with the Israeli defense minister and claimed that Hussein was not a threat to Israel. Bob urged President Bush to sell wheat to Iraq and described Saddam as "a leader to whom the United States can talk." Four months later, Dole's buddy Saddam invaded Kuwait.

- In 1996, Dole kicked off his presidential campaign stops with a version of the 1967 hit "Soul Man" changed to read "Dole Man." The company that owned the song sued the campaign, and "Dole Man" was pulled from use. Bob's handlers then began playing the Elton John song "I'm Still Standing" after Dole fell off the stage at a campaign stop.

- In his later years, Dole became a TV pitchman. He appeared in ads for SuperTarget stores in which he declared that he remained committed to giving voters a choice: "Paper or plastic?"

- Dole was hired as a pitchman for Dunkin' Donuts, even though he hated such junk food. "Lotsa fat. Lotsa calories," Dole grumped. "I've been eating low-fat stuff."

- Bob and Liddy Dole owned an apartment at the Watergate building right next to Monica Lewinsky's. Dole distributed free Dunkin' Donuts to reporters camped outside her door and later bought her apartment.

- Bob Dole participated in clinical trials for Viagra. He later became a national spokesperson for the product, educating the public about "E.D."—erectile dysfunction. At one point, he told the press that with Viagra, his brains were in his crotch.

- While talking to the *New York Times* about Liddy's run for the presidency in 2000, Dole all-but-endorsed his wife's rival, Sen. John McCain (R-Arizona). "I think we need to keep good people in the race," Bob said, "so I've thought about ways to help McCain." Dick Armey, the House Republican majority leader, quipped, "He's going to be singing 'Strangers in the Night' for a long time."

Bob Dornan

DUMBEST QUOTES

"The best compliment I've ever had on the House floor—now brace yourself—was from Henry Hyde [R-Illinois]. . . . He goes, 'Dornan, we decided that if we were Indians in the Plains Wars and you were a cavalry trooper, we would kill you just to cut out your heart and eat it.' And I said, 'Now wait a minute, run that by me one more time. Okay, I guess that's a compliment. Thanks.' And they meant it as a compliment. *No, no, no, no!* I turned it into an Aztec thing, too much. What Henry said was, 'If we were Indians in the Plains Wars and you were a cavalry trooper, we would kill you just to drink your blood.' And that sounds a little better than 'cut your heart out.' And of course, this is what Indians did do in lots of primitive cultures, when they really respected a warrior. . . . So I really rate that as the nicest compliment I've had yet."

FACTS OF LIFE

ORIGIN: Born Robert Kenneth Owen Dornan, April 3, 1933, New York City, New York.

FORMATIVE YEARS: Loyola Marymount University, studied drama from 1950 to 1953, then dropped out.

FAMILY PLANNING: Married Sallie Hansen, 1955.

SELECTED ELECTION SCORECARD: 1976–82: won, U.S. House of Representatives, 27th District, California. 1982: lost, U.S. Senate, California. 1984–92: won, U.S. House of Representatives, 38th District, California. 1996: lost, U. S. president. 1993–96: won, U.S. House of Representatives, 46th District, California. 1996–98: lost, U.S. House of Representatives, 46th District, California.

QUICKIE BIO

He's just a nasty man," declared one of Dornan's political rivals. "As nasty a person as you can imagine." He was the son of a former Ziegfeld Follies showgirl and nephew of the actor (Jack Haley) who played the Tin Man in the children's film classic *The Wizard of Oz* (1939). Bob Dornan grew up on the streets of New York, moved to Southern California, dropped out of college to join the air force, then mustered out and settled in Los Angeles where he became a cab driver, a gym teacher, and an actor. The red-haired, loud-mouthed "Mad Dog" Dornan appeared in the 1960s TV series *Twelve O'Clock High, Bewitched,* and *I Dream of Jeannie,* and in several movies, including *Hell on Wheels* (1967) and *To the Shores of Hell* (1967), as well as hosting TV and radio programs in the Los Angeles area. Dissatisfied with his show biz career, Dornan entered politics, turned on the Hollywood crowd, and became Congress' leading gay basher. Dornan, whose district included Disneyland, served more than a decade in Congress, but seemed to have spent too much time in fantasyland. Bob once snarled, "Every lesbian spear-chucker in this country is hoping I get defeated." Eventually, he was.

BOB DORNAN DOES THE DUMBEST THINGS

✪ Dornan liked to brag about his combat service record and referred to himself as a "s***-hot fighter pilot." However, he never actually flew in combat, although he did manage to crash planes and a helicopter.

✪ On the day after Halloween in 1984, Dornan and a group appeared at his Democratic Congressional opponent's headquarters. Bob wore Groucho Marx glasses and his followers wore red cat suits. A fight ensued, and three police cars were summoned to break up the scuffle.

✪ Dornan once attacked an episode of the award winning TV show *Masterpiece Theatre* as "a training ground for lesbians." At least twice he attacked supporters of an opponent as "lesbian spear-chuckers."

✪ In January 1995, Dornan called Pres. Bill Clinton a "flawed human being" and a "draft-dodging adulterer not fit to lace the boots" of the military personnel under his command. Bob described Clinton's exercise regimen the following way: "The Commander-in-Chief is jogging in San Francisco in his slit-up-the-sides silk girlie-girlie jogging pants showing us those beautiful white doughboy thighs of his."

✪ Describing men who were pro-choice on the abortion issue, Dornan declared, "These are either women trapped in men's bodies, . . . or younger guys who are camp followers looking for easy sex."

★ The former actor Dornan declared that Hollywood had "polluted the spiritual and moral climate of our country." After seeing the explicit movie *Basic Instinct* (1992), Bob asked, "How many people are going to emulate now, trying to go to high school like Sharon Stone, with no underwear on because she uncrossed her legs in front of five detectives?"

★ During his unsuccessful run for U.S. Senate in 1982, Bob accused his opponent, Republican Barry Goldwater Jr., of attending a get together at the Playboy mansion, where, Dornan claimed, partygoers regularly indulged in bestiality.

★ On a commercial airline flight in 1991, Dornan reportedly refused to put his seat into an upright position before takeoff, got into a dispute with a flight attendant, and was asked to leave the plane.

★ On the floor of the House, Rep. Thomas Downey (D-New York) asked Bob if he had ever called him a "draft-dodging wimp." A furious Dornan grabbed Downey by the collar and tie and allegedly threatened him with "bodily harm." Dornan later gave the wimpy explanation that he was merely trying to straighten a knot in Downey's tie.

★ Bob ran for president in 1996. He finished dead last in the New Hampshire primary—officially receiving zero percent of the vote. He even finished behind Sen. Phil Gramm (R-Texas) who had officially dropped out of the race months before. Still Dornan persevered. He spent so much time running for president that he neglected his Congressional reelection campaign and lost it.

★ After losing his Congressional seat in 1996, Dornan claimed voter fraud. He also stated, "What beat me was more homosexual money than in any race in history, including from a group called Lesbians for Motherhood." Later, the former congressman walked onto the floor of the House and threatened Rep. Robert Menendez (D-New Jersey). Reportedly, Dornan called Menendez a coward, shouted profanity, and suggested they step outside to settle their differences. For his hot-headed action, Bob became the first former House member ever to be banned from the House floor.

David Duke

FACTS OF LIFE

ORIGIN: Born David Ernest Duke, July 1, 1950, Tulsa, Oklahoma.

FORMATIVE YEARS: Louisiana State University, B.A. 1974.

FAMILY PLANNING: Married Chloe Hardin (waitress), September 9, 1972; divorced, 1984.

SELECTED ELECTION SCORECARD: 1990: lost, U.S. Senate, Louisiana. 1991: lost, governor, Louisiana. 1992: lost, U.S. president. 1996: lost, U.S. Senate, Louisiana. 1998: lost, U.S. House of Representatives, 1st District, Louisiana.

QUICKIE BIO

Only in America could a former Grand Wizard of the Ku Klux Klan and a fervent Nazi run for public office as a born-again Christian and win. Or maybe only in Louisiana. Born to a conservative oil company engineer, David was known to his schoolmates as "Puke Duke" or "Duke Puke." Even his mother couldn't stand him. She told her friends she "must have gotten ahold of the wrong child." David Duke grabbed onto right wing politics in high school, wore swastikas around the Louisiana State University campus, and made a living peddling Nazi and racist literature while grabbing as much of the political spotlight as he could. In the 1970s, Duke traveled the country to promote the Ku Klux Klan, then left the KKK in 1982 to found the National Association for the Advancement of White People (NAAWP). He disappeared from public view for a few years, then declared himself a Republican and stunned the nation by winning election to the Louisiana State House of Representatives in 1988. Luckily for most everyone, Duke was defeated in later elections, although he managed to pick up a large percentage of the white vote in his home county. After losing his presidential bid, Duke peddled his newsletters and leftover racist political paraphernalia at collectors' memorabilia shows. "He looked sort of pitiful," recalled one witness. "No one was paying attention to him."

DAVID DUKE DOES
THE DUMBEST THINGS

✪ Duke traveled to Laos to teach English in 1971. He was fired when his boss found him teaching the Laotian soldiers how to make Molotov cocktails.

✪ In 1971, Duke confronted left-wing radical Jerry Rubin after Rubin spoke to the students at Louisiana State University. "Jerry Rubin!" Duke yelled, "aren't you that big, tough Jew Revolutionary? Jerry, you've got a fascist right in front of you! Why don't you show your followers how tough you are?" Duke later bragged, "It was the most hilarious thing you ever saw."

✪ David was arrested in 1972 for soliciting money for the George Wallace campaign and, allegedly, pocketing it for himself.

✪ In 1974, David appeared on Tom Snyder's TV program *Tomorrow*. "I'd always thought of the Klan as being a bunch of old fogies who were concerned with yesterday," Snyder enthused. "But you're intelligent, articulate, charming."

✪ Two years later, Duke burned a cross in Louisiana at the conclusion of a Klan convention and was arrested for inciting a riot. He was found guilty.

✪ In 1978, David traveled to Great Britain to recruit new Klan members. When it was discovered that he was in the country, there were yells for his expulsion, but a high ranking official declared, "I don't intend to use the powers I have to crack a nut." The bureaucrat finally signed an order for Duke's deportation, but David eluded capture. He wore his Klan robes around London and had his photo taken standing next to the red-uniformed Beefeaters. He went to a pub for an interview. The reporter called Scotland Yard, but when the authorities arrived, they arrested the journalist, not Duke. David ran down an alley, but was apprehended and dragged away shouting, "God Save the Queen."

✪ At a Klan leadership meeting in 1979, Duke promised attendees a big surprise at the event finale. Everyone gazed at the stage as the curtain rose to reveal—David Duke, topless in shorts, lifting weights to display his rippling muscles. According to one witness, "It was all some people could do to avoid laughing."

★ Duke claimed that he was trying to turn the Klan into a "movement of love."

★ To make some quick cash, David wrote a self-defense manual for blacks entitled *African Atto*. Using the pseudonym Mohammed X, Duke wrote: "African Atto can only be effectively used by black people. Just as whites can't 'soul dance' as well as our people, so they can never use this skill as well either." One of the secrets of the how-to guide was that black fighters should yell "Hootoo!" to rid their bodies of "bad air."

★ Duke also wrote a sex guide for women entitled *Finders-Keepers*. Under the pseudonym Dorothy Vanderbilt, David urged his female readers to engage in anal and oral sex. "That's quite a bedtime snack," Duke-as-Vanderbilt observed. "At least it's low on calories."

★ Duke enjoyed numerous sexual exploits of his own. A prostitute claimed that she was urged by a friend to have sex with the Grand Dragon. According to the woman, Duke undressed, lay on the bed, and said, "Do what you will, I only want to please you." Then he said, "Pretend that it's a vanilla ice-cream cone, honey." "Not chocolate, right?" the woman quipped. David claimed, "The woman is totally off her rocker."

★ David enjoyed taking friends to the Western Sizzler steakhouse in Metairie, Louisiana. He often ordered the most expensive steak, then went from table to table saying, "I'm David Duke, and I'm the head of the NAAWP. Can you make a donation?" It is rumored that, supposedly, he usually got enough money to pay his bill, with change left over.

★ Before he entered politics in the late 1980s, Duke reportedly had a nose job, a chin implant, and two facial chemical peels. When asked in 1991 by a TV reporter if he had ever had a chemical face peel, David Duke exploded, "That's the kind of cheap shot a little worm like you would make. . . . You could use a little plastic surgery yourself."

★ In 1986, Duke took his girlfriend on a romantic vacation to Europe to visit a concentration camp in Germany. "This could not possibly have been a gas chamber because it was too small," tour guide Duke insisted. "Some people did die, yes. But there was no official order to kill Jews."

★ Duke claimed that "the concentration camps were myths concocted by Hollywood to help create the state of Israel." "You know, they had a soccer field at Auschwitz. They had a swimming pool at Auschwitz. They had an orchestra at Auschwitz. . . . The band was for the prisoners' enjoyment, pleasure."

★ Duke told a reporter that the Nazis were environmental utopians who had "a real sense of unity with nature and believing in non-pollution and relocating factories in the countryside and creating a whole community around nature walks . . ."

★ Whenever he watched the TV sitcom program *Hogan's Heroes,* set in a World War II Nazi concentration camp, Duke yelled at the producers for making the Nazis look bad.

★ Duke was a compulsive gambler who loved to shoot craps. When he ran for U.S. Senate in 1990, he denied that he was a gaming enthusiast and claimed that he went to Las Vegas because "I like to go hiking in the desert."

★ In 1991, David Duke campaigned for governor of Louisiana against the twice-indicted, never-convicted, former Gov. Edwin Edwards. Like Duke, Edwards loved the betting game of craps. Edwards bragged to voters about another skill he shared with David: "We're both wizards under the sheets." Edwards won the election, but Duke won the white vote.

Gerald Ford
All-American Presidential Bonus Chapter

FACTS OF LIFE

ORIGIN: Born Leslie Lynch King Jr., July 14, 1913, Omaha, Nebraska. (His mother later remarried and Leslie was adopted and given the name Gerald [Jerry] Rudolph Ford Jr.)

FORMATIVE YEARS: University of Michigan, B.A. 1935; Yale Law School, J.D. 1941.

FAMILY PLANNING: Married Elizabeth "Betty" Bloomer Warren (model, dance teacher), 1948.

SELECTED ELECTION SCORECARD: 1948–73: won, U.S. House of Representatives, 5th District, Michigan. 1973: appointed U.S. vice president (after the resignation of Spiro Agnew). 1974: appointed U.S. president (after the resignation of Pres. Richard M. Nixon). 1976: lost, U.S. president.

QUICKIE BIO

Gerald Ford was an accidental president, who became known as the president who had accidents. He was the first chief executive to hold the top two posts in the American government without having been elected to either of them, and the first man ever to be appointed to the U.S. Presidency. Ford's entire life followed a similarly blessed but circuitous path. When Ford was just a toddler, his mother left his abusive biological father, moved back in with her parents in Grand Rapids, Michigan, divorced and remarried. Ford grew up to be a model youth, an Eagle Scout, and an All-American football player at the University of Michigan. Gerald became an actual model in 1939, the only U.S. president to date to hold that distinction, when he and his girl-friend Phyllis Brown were featured in a *Look* magazine article about the lives of the "beautiful people." Ford turned down pro football contracts, and went to Yale where he studied law and helped coach the football team. After join-ing the navy and seeing fierce combat in World War II, Ford returned to his law practice in Michigan, married, was asked to run for Congress, and won— for the next twenty-five years. The congressman known as "Mr. Nice Guy," who described himself as "disgustingly sane," was married to a woman who was not quite so together. After partying it up as First Lady, Betty Ford went for treatment at a California substance abuse treatment center. The facility near Palm Springs, which today bears her name, became a celebrity hangout, serving clients that included Pres. Jimmy Carter's brother, Billy. As for Jerry, who graduated near the top of his class at Yale, his legacy seemed to be that of a presidential goofball. After industrialist Justin Dart said hello to then ex-Pres. Gerald Ford on a plane, Dart turned to a reporter and told him, "Jerry's a nice man, but he's not very smart. Actually, our seatmate is a dumb bastard." The president best known for his continual pratfalls was smart enough to write an autobiography. The title? *A Time to Heal.*

GERALD FORD DOES
THE DUMBEST THINGS

✪ Pres. Lyndon Johnson complained that Ford had "played football too long without a helmet." In 1968, Ford reacted to the comment by taking one of his old football helmets to the Gridiron Dinner. When he had trouble putting on the helmet, he explained, "Heads tend to swell in Washington."

✪ Lyndon Johnson said that Jerry Ford was "so dumb he can't walk and fart at the same time." When Ford opposed one of President Johnson's Model Cities programs, LBJ instructed an assistant, "Joe, you've got a little baby boy. Well, you take his little building blocks and go up and explain to Jerry Ford what we're trying to do."

✪ Richard Nixon laughed at the idea of Ford being president. Sitting in the Oval Office he joked, "Can you imagine him sitting in this chair?" When

Gerald Ford had the reputation of being a klutz, but he managed to "pass the straw" successfully in 1974 at a restaurant in Korea.
(Courtesy of Gerald R. Ford Library)

he appointed Ford vice president, Nixon said that he could use Ford as his "tool" and that all he had to do was "wind him up and he'll go 'arf, arf.' "

✪ On September 8, 1974, one month after taking office, Ford granted President Nixon an unconditional pardon for all alleged federal crimes that Nixon had "committed or may have committed or taken part in." When Ford dodged questions about Nixon's complicity in the Watergate scandal, a reporter commented that his words were "zigs and zags." Ex-all-American gridironer Ford offered, "A zig-zagger makes touchdowns."

✪ President Ford was eating dinner with his family in Vail, Colorado, when his dog pooped on the floor. A White House steward rushed over to clean up the mess. Gerald got up, took the rag from the steward and finished the task, saying, "No man should have to clean up after another man's dog."

✪ Ford kept a pet golden retriever at the White House named Liberty. The dog usually slept outside, but she was expecting puppies, so her trainer was keeping her inside. One night the trainer had to go out, and the president agreed to let the dog sleep in his room. The canine woke up and licked his face. The president dutifully walked the dog outside, then locked himself out of the White House. Ford wandered around the building, pounding on doors. The Secret Service finally woke up, and let the president back in.

✪ In 1975, Air Force One arrived in Salzburg, Austria. The Chief Executive stepped out of the plane, slipped, fell down the exit ramp, landed on the runway, and jumped up unhurt. White House photographer David Kennerly joked, "Nice of you to drop in." Later that same day, Gerald slipped twice on the staircase at a Salzburg palace.

✪ Comedian Chevy Chase spoofed Ford's falls and slips on the TV comedy/variety program *Saturday Night Live*. The president defended himself by saying, "I'm an activist. Activists are more prone to stumble than anyone else."

✪ In the early days of his presidency, Ford got annoyed when the media reported that he was "acting presidential," "assuming a presidential posture," and "trying to look presidential." Gerald made a point of telling the press that he was not "acting presidential." He *was* the president. "I don't look very good," he emphasized later, "but I'm a darned good president."

✪ The press always seemed to be catching Ford entangled in the leashes of his dogs, bumping his head on the door of his helicopter, falling down on skis, or being locked out of his own news conference. He was depicted as Bozo the Clown on the cover of *New York* magazine and the popular journal hailed him as "Our Top Fall-Down Comic," and "The Great Blub Dub." Ford was good-natured about the ribbing but sometimes sighed, "I get so tired of this horses***!"

✪ When he was really angry at someone, Ford exclaimed, "He doesn't know his ass from page eight!" No one knew what he was talking about.

✪ After Ford hosted entertainer Vicki Carr one evening at the White House, the red hot Mexican-American singer asked the president, "What's your favorite Mexican dish?" Ford's answer? "You are."

✪ Betty Ford kept a close eye on her husband. When she caught him ogling a pretty girl on a presidential trip, she hissed, "Jerry!" On a trip to Helsinki, Finland, Ford was particularly impressed by the local women. Ford flirted with one in particular and mentioned her to his aides. Leaving Helsinki, a staff member commented that he would like to return sometime. The president quipped, "The next time, we will come without the ladies." Betty snapped, "The hell you will!"

✪ "The three-martini lunch is the epitome of American efficiency," Gerald Ford proclaimed once. "Where else can you get an earful, a bellyful, and a snootful at the same time?"

✪ Inspired perhaps by the yellow smiley face buttons, Ford decided that the best way to fix the ailing American economy was to distribute buttons that said WIN for "Whip Inflation Now."

✪ While discussing a School Lunch bill, Ford offered, "I strongly support the feeding of children."

✪ At a reception in Omaha, Nebraska, a little old lady came up to President Ford and said, "I hear you spoke here tonight." The humble president replied, "Oh, it was nothing." "Yes," wheezed the woman, "that's what I heard."

✪ Ford couldn't dodge the bullets from the press, but he could dodge assassins' bullets. In September 1975, Lynette Alice "Squeaky" Fromme, a follower of Charles Manson, pointed a loaded pistol at Ford and fired. Luckily the chamber was empty. Seventeen days later in San Francisco, Sarah Jane Moore shot a pistol at Ford, and just missed. A bystander named Oliver Sipple jumped in the way, and threw Moore to the ground as the gun went off.

✪ A lot of Ford's accidents were actually due to things beyond his control. For example, when asked for a comment on Pope Paul VI's birthday in 1974, his Secretary of Agriculture Earl L. Butz cracked, "He no play-a da game, he no make-a da rules."

✪ At a cabinet meeting, Butz told a joke about a fly who kept falling off the handle of a pitchfork into a pile of manure. The punch line? "Don't fly off the handle when you're full of s***." President Ford groaned, "Oh, come on Earl."

✪ During the 1976 presidential campaign, Butz was flying on a plane next to Nixon White House official-turned-reporter John Dean, entertainer Sonny Bono, and singer Pat Boone. Butz told the boys a joke about a dog having sex with a skunk. Boone asked Butz why the Republican Party did not attract more African-American support. Butz reportedly replied that the "coloreds" only wanted three things. "First, a tight p***y; second, loose shoes; and, third, a warm place to s***." Butz resigned soon after making the comment.

✪ During the 1976 presidential campaign debate with Jimmy Carter, Ford announced, "There is no Soviet domination of Eastern Europe and there never will be under the Ford administration." Oops! A few days later, Ford declared, "We are going to make certain to the best of our ability that any allegation of domination is not a fact."

★ At one hotel, Ford was given the Emperor Suite. He asked his staff to change the name emblazoned on the door. Soon the nameplate was covered by a piece of cardboard on which someone scrawled with a felt-tip pen, "Jerry Ford's Room."

★ The final ten days of Jerry's 1976 campaign were dubbed by members of his staff as a "ten-day orgasm." He drove in a limo with loudspeakers hidden in the fenders so he could talk to crowds along the campaign route. Most observers were startled rather than interested in what they heard. The vehicle became known as "The Amazing Talking Car."

★ On ABC-TV's *Monday Night Baseball* in 1978, Ford admitted, "I watch a lot of baseball on radio."

★ At the 1995 Bob Hope Golf Classic, Gerald Ford hit a spectator with a ball. Hope claimed that Ford was the only golfer he'd ever known who lost a ball in the ball washer.

Bonus Chapter
Gay (and Gay-Bashing) Republicans

QUICKIE OVERVIEW

"These people are intellectually dishonest in just everything they say or do," Sen. Jesse Helms (R-North Carolina) has declared. "They start by pretending that it is just another form of love. It's sickening," he adds. A gay person is not necessarily dumb. But a gay Republican? Well, maybe, a gay Republican is not necessarily dumb, either. What is dumb is the fact that Republicans spend so much time talking about gays that some might think G.O.P. stands for Gay Old Party. It's dumb enough for Republicans to bash gays. But it's really dumb for Republicans to bash gays who vote Republican. Organizations like the Log Cabin Republicans have tried to help the Republicans come to terms with their own sexuality. But such organizations have a long way to go. "If a person is still living a lifestyle that is an offense to God, there's no room to recognize them in the party," Rep. Bob Dornan (R-California) snarled. "I hope my party never officially recognizes groups that are based upon observable offenses against God and the natural order." Oh, Bobby, behave!

GAY (AND GAY-BASHING) REPUBLICANS DO THE DUMBEST THINGS

✪ Who was the first U.S. congressman to die of AIDS in office? Rep. Stewart B. McKinney (R-Connecticut), who succumbed to the disease in 1987. Republicans claimed that McKinney contracted AIDS from a blood transfusion he received during heart surgery in 1979. The *Washington Post*, however, claimed that McKinney, who was married and had two kids, was homosexual. Of course, according to Sen. Jesse Helms (R-North Carolina), "The *New York Times* and the *Washington Post* are both infested with homosexuals themselves."

✪ Sen. Jesse Helms opposed the appointment of Roberta Achtenburg as Assistant Secretary in the Department of Housing and Urban Development. Why? Helms explained, "I'm not going to put a damn lesbian in a position like that. If you want to call me a bigot, fine."

✪ When asked in 1967 if homosexuals should be barred from public office, Gov. Ronald Reagan of California quipped, "Certainly they should be barred from the Department of Beaches and Parks."

✪ President Richard Nixon (R-California) believed that homosexuality had a huge negative impact on world history. "You know what happened to the Greeks?" Nixon asked his White House assistants. "Homosexuality destroyed them." Nixon went on to observe, "The Catholic Church went to hell three or four centuries ago. It was homosexual, and it had to be cleaned out." Commenting on San Francisco's gay community, the chief executive sighed, "I can't shake hands with anybody from San Francisco."

✪ Sen. Orrin Hatch (R-Utah) declared to a group of Utah Republicans that he was proud that "we don't have the gays and lesbians with us." Later he said that "homosexuality is contrary to the Bible," but acknowledged that he was "tolerant of all people." Hatch also described the Democratic Party as "the Party of homosexuals."

✪ In 1994, Rep. Steve C. Gunderson (R-Wisconsin) addressed a Human Rights Campaign Fund and, according to reporters, left the impression that he was gay. During a debate on the House floor a few days later, fellow politician Bob Dornan addressed Gunderson about his position on a bill and declared, "I guess you're out because you went up and spoke to a large homosexual dinner, Mr. Gunderson." Dornan later spoke with a reporter and reportedly called Gunderson a "homo."

✪ A group of gay activists once confronted the gay-bashing Dornan and his wife Sallie. In the middle of the confrontation, Sallie shocked everyone present when she announced that her brother had AIDS. Dornan later claimed that he had been in the dark. Equally in the dark was Sallie's brother, who denied that he had AIDS.

✪ In 1983, Pat Buchanan commented on AIDS by saying, "The poor homosexuals—they have declared war on nature, and now nature is exacting an awful retribution." At a Dartmouth College rally nine years later, Buchanan denied that he had said AIDS was "God's retribution" against homosexuals, and claimed that he had described AIDS as "*nature's* retribution" against homosexuals.

✪ Gov. Edwin Mecham (R-Arizona) asked for a list of all homosexuals in the state government. In July 1987, Edwin accused the "homosexual lobby" of being out to get him and stated flat out, "Don't ever ask me for a true statement again." Mecham was later impeached and convicted, and left office.

✪ Rep. Sonny Bono (R-California) supported the Defense of Marriage Act proposed by Rep. Bob Barr (R-Georgia). The act specifically banned same-sex marriages. Chastity Bono, Bono's daughter who is a lesbian and a lesbian activist, commented, "While he has had gays and lesbians working for him and has always appeared accepting of me, his voting record on gay and lesbian issues has been totally atrocious. How can I respect him for that?" Bono explained his anti-gay vote by saying, "I simply can't handle it."

✪ In the spring of 1999, California State Senator William J. Knight led a campaign to ban same-sex marriages in his home state. Three years earlier, Knight had announced that his brother, John, was gay and had died of AIDS, and that his son, David, was also gay. "His is a blind, uncaring, uninformed, knee-jerk reaction to a subject about which he knows nothing and wants to know nothing," son David said of his father. David further declared that Knight had become fiercely anti-gay because it served his political career.

✪ After Texas billionaire (and founder of the Reform Party) Ross Perot acquired the Wall Street investment firm DuPont Glore Forgan, he encountered an employee of the company who was wearing a blue shirt. Perot chuckled, "I don't know whether to kiss him or shake his hand." Ross referred to men who wore blue shirts as "sissies." The company quickly went bankrupt.

✪ In 1992, Perot claimed that that he had gay employees who were "brilliant people, doing outstanding work." A short time later, Ross declared that "as far as he knew" he had never met a gay person.

✪ Sen. Jesse Helms (R-North Carolina) described homosexuals as "weak, morally sick wretches." In 1977, he became an enthusiastic backer of former Miss America Anita Bryant who launched a campaign against a homosexual rights ordinance in Dade County, Florida. Bryant described homosexuals as "human garbage." Four years later, Bryant divorced her husband, and opened a dress shop. When asked about the large number of gays in the fashion world, Anita said it didn't matter. "Anyway," Helms's former ally observed, "I can't tell who's gay and who isn't."

✪ Rep. Bob Bauman (R-Maryland) was the founder and national chairman of the Young Americans for Freedom, the head of the American Conservative Union, and a leader of the moral majority who was vehemently anti-gay. But Bauman liked to cruise "over and under" gay bars in Washington, where the clients were either over forty or under twenty-five, and referred to his young boyfriends as "twinkies." Bauman also liked to pick up male hustlers while driving around in his large sedan with the Maryland state seal on the license plates and the words, "Member of Congress 1." Four weeks before the 1980 Congressional elections, Bauman was busted for allegedly soliciting sex in a gay bar with a nude male dancer. Another man came forth and claimed that he had had an affair with the gay-bashing Bauman. Bob admitted that he had "homosexual tendencies" and lost the election.

✪ In 1976, Jon Hinson worked as an administrative assistant for Rep. Thad Cochran (R-Mississippi). Apparently, Hinson liked to pick up guys at the Iwo Jima Memorial (for the World War II battle in the Pacific) in the nation's capitol. He was busted in a park on a charge of allegedly committing an obscene act, but the charge was later dropped. The next year, a fire broke out in a gay Washington movie house. Hinson was one of three customers who survived. Jon was elected to the House of Representatives in 1978. In 1980, he was running for reelection when he stunned supporters at a press conference in Mississippi by declaring that he was gay. Hinson argued that it was "better to just get it out there and hope people understood." They did and he won reelection.

✪ However, the next year Jon Hinson was caught in the Longworth "Tea Room," a bathroom facility on Capitol Hill, sipping "tea" with a twenty-eight-year-old staffer from the Library of Congress. Hinson resigned from office.

✪ Gov. George W. Bush (R-Texas) declared his opposition to allowing gay and lesbian couples to adopt kids. Later, George W. approached Texas state representative Glen Maxey (D-Texas), hugged him, and said, "Glen, I value you as a person and as a human being. I want you to know, Glen, that no matter what I say publicly about gay people, it does not pertain to you personally." Maxey untwined himself from George's embrace and responded, "Governor, when you say a gay person isn't fit to be a parent, you're talking about me. It is personal."

✪ "Yes it is," Sen. Trent Lott (R-Mississippi) responded when asked if homosexuality was a sin. But Lott did express hope for homosexuals. "Others have a sex addiction or are kleptomaniacs. There are all kinds of problems and addictions and difficulties and experiences that are wrong."

✪ In June 1988, a group of gay Republicans called the Log Cabin Republicans tried to set up a booth at the Texas State Republican convention in Fort Worth. Officials refused to let the group do so and a party spokesman likened the organization to the Ku Klux Klan and child molesters. Outside the convention, anti-gay demonstrators waved signs saying, "There's no such thing as a Christian fag." However, it should be noted that Richard Tafel, the head of the Log Cabin Republicans at that time, was an American Baptist minister.

✪ In December 1999, the Vermont Supreme Court decided to recognize same-sex marriages. Republican presidential primary candidate Gary Bauer immediately declared, "I think what the Vermont Supreme Court did last week was the worst form of terrorism." Worse than terrorist bombings?

Newt Gingrich

FACTS OF LIFE

ORIGIN: Born Newton Leroy McPherson, June 17, 1943, Harrisburg, Pennsylvania (adopted by Robert Gingrich).

FORMATIVE YEARS: Emory University, B.A. 1965; Tulane University, Ph.D. 1971.

FAMILY PLANNING: Married Jackie Battley (teacher), 1962; divorced, 1980; married Marianne Ginther (community planner), August 1981; divorced, 1999.

SELECTED ELECTION SCORECARD: 1974–76: lost, U.S. House of Representatives, 6th District, Georgia. 1978–98: won, U.S. House of Representatives, 6th District, Georgia.

QUICKIE BIO

My enemies will dismiss me. My friends will write histories that glorify me. And two or three generations from now, some historian will write a history that implies I was whoever I was." Abandoned by his father and raised by a manic-depressive mother, Newt reportedly smoked pot in college, refused to get a job, begged tuition money from his parents, got a doctorate in history, and landed a teaching gig at West Georgia College near Atlanta. Newt ran for Congress from suburban Atlanta, and realized his dream of becoming "an old time political boss." But his snarling, meanspirited brand of politics became such a joke that folks said Newt gave newts a bad name. In

1994, Newt became the Speaker of the U.S. House of Representatives, the first Republican in forty years to hold that title. Four years later, he resigned from office to become a visionary. And what was his vision? According to his mother, "Newtie was always for Newtie."

NEWT GINGRICH DOES
THE DUMBEST THINGS

⭐ "I don't want to go to work," graduate student Newt complained to his stepmother when he asked her for money. Years later, Professor Newt declared, "I personally favor mandatory requirement of work for everybody, including women with small children."

⭐ In his lecture series "Renewing American Civilization," Gingrich observed, "If combat means living in a ditch, females have biological problems staying in a ditch for thirty days because they get infections. . . . On the other hand, men are basically little piglets: you drop them in a ditch, they roll around in it—it doesn't matter, you know. These things are very real."

⭐ Newt could stop the government, but he couldn't kill a hog. In the 1970s, he and his buddy decided to barbecue a hog in Gingrich's driveway. Newt demanded that he be the one to shoot the hog between the eyes. At the last second, he flinched, missed the shot, and wounded the hog on the side of the head. The animal ran away. Instead of going after it, Gingrich called the hog to come back to him. "You just shot the son of a bitch in the head, Newt," his buddy said, "why do you think he's gonna come to you?" The pal had to put the hog out of its misery.

⭐ Newt's first wife was his high school geometry teacher. They married when he was nineteen and she was twenty-six. But during his first run for Congress in 1974, Newt began straying from his wedding vows with a young campaign worker. According to Kip Carter, his campaign treasurer, "We'd have won in 1974 if we could have kept him out of the office, screwing her on the desk."

⭐ One evening, Kip Carter was accompanying Jackie Sue and Kathy, Newt's two daughters, after a football game at the college where Gingrich taught. "I was cutting across the yard to go up the driveway," Carter recalled. "There was a car there. As I got to the car, I saw Newt in the passenger seat and one of the guys' wives with her head in his lap going up and down. Newt kind of turned and gave me his little-boy smile. Fortunately, Jackie Sue and Kathy were a lot younger and shorter then."

★ Anne Manning was the wife of one of Newt's academic colleagues and a campaign worker during his unsuccessful 1976 campaign. One night in the spring of 1977, Manning ended up at a Washington hotel with Gingrich. "We had oral sex," Manning declared. "He prefers that modus operandi because then he can say, 'I never slept with her.' " Even so, the married Newt supposedly threatened, "If you ever tell anybody about this, I'll say you're lying."

★ In January 1980, Gingrich met the future Mrs. Newt II, Marianne Ginther. Later that spring, his then wife was diagnosed with uterine cancer. He visited her in the hospital after her third surgery, but not primarily to sympathize with her. He basically wanted to discuss divorce terms.

★ When Newt was three, his biological dad allowed his stepfather to adopt him in exchange for not having to pay four months of child support. Gingrich followed in his father's deadbeat footsteps. Newt's wife Jackie reportedly had to go to court to get enough money from him to pay the utility bills for herself and his daughters. The story made the papers before the 1980 election, but Newt still won. One staffer developed the theory that Gingrich won the votes of "angry white males . . . who felt trashed by women."

★ After the assassination of Israeli Prime Minister Yitzhak Rabin in 1995, Newt climbed aboard Air Force One to attend the funeral. On the flight over and back, Gingrich sat in a different part of the plane from President Clinton and his Democratic entourage and had to leave the plane by a different exit than the president. "Where's their sense of manners?" Newt complained. "Where's their sense of courtesy?"

★ Newt was so angry about being slighted on the flight that he stonewalled the negotiations for the federal budget in 1995, forcing the government to shut down. "I'm going to say up front it's petty," Gingrich bragged as the government ground to a halt. "But I think it's human."

★ Gingrich strongly believed in freedom. "A mere forty years ago, beach volley ball was just beginning," Newt announced at the 1996 Republican convention. "No bureaucrat could have invented it, and that's what freedom's all about."

★ Newt declared that more orphanages might help maintain the American social order.

★ Newt's second wife, Marianne, tried to keep him happy by wearing bows in her hair and becoming an image consultant for BeautiControl Cosmetics. As a birthday surprise, she even gave him an emerald-tree boa.

They kept the snake in the bathtub. Newt said the chances of the marriage succeeding were fifty-three to forty-seven.

★ When Marianne once asked Newt to take out the garbage, he explained that he was on the phone talking about the situation in Nicaragua. "Lives are at stake here," the congressman declared. "It doesn't matter," his second wife insisted. "Take the garbage out."

★ When actress Melanie Griffith came to Washington, D.C. and the Capitol building to lobby for the National Endowment for the Arts, she happened to bump into Newt Gingrich in the hallway. Gingrich looked at the hot actress and asked, "Do you want to see my dinosaur?" He was probably talking about the dinosaur bone he kept in his office.

★ Newt reportedly had numerous "breakfast meetings" with a female staff member of the House Agricultural Committee as early as 1995. While supposedly sewing his wild oats with the staffer, the married Gingrich berated unwed mothers, urged sexual abstinence, and led the campaign to impeach President Clinton for womanizing.

★ After resigning his Congressional seat in 1998, and divorcing his second wife in 2000, fifty-something old Newt enjoyed spending his now free evenings with the thirty-three-year-old agricultural bureaucrat.

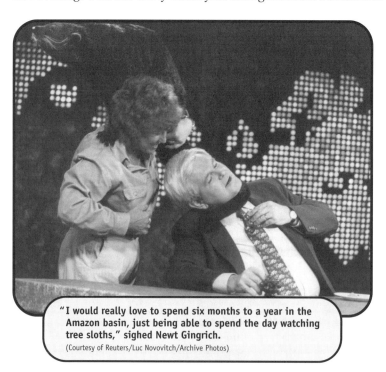

"I would really love to spend six months to a year in the Amazon basin, just being able to spend the day watching tree sloths," sighed Newt Gingrich.
(Courtesy of Reuters/Luc Novovitch/Archive Photos)

Rudolph Giuliani

FACTS OF LIFE

ORIGIN: Born Rudolph William Giuliani, May 28, 1944, Brooklyn, New York.

FORMATIVE YEARS: Manhattan College, B.A. 1965; New York University Law School, J.D. 1968.

FAMILY PLANNING: Married Donna Hanover (TV anchorwoman), 1984.

SELECTED ELECTION SCORECARD: 1989: lost, mayor, New York City. 1994–98: won, mayor, New York City. 2000: potential candidate U.S. Senate.

QUICKIE BIO

As a sensational prosecuting attorney in New York City, Rudolph Giuliani took on Carmine "The Snake" Persico, Anthony "Fat Tony" Salerno, Anthony "Tony Ducks" Corallo, and other big name Mafia operators. As the 107th mayor of the Big Apple, Giuliani took on jaywalkers, taxi drivers, and street vendors, and was dubbed the Mussolini of New York City. The grandson of Italian immigrants, Giuliani was born in Brooklyn to a bar and grill owner. He attended Catholic schools through college. He considered becoming a priest until he went on a retreat with other monks, and, thereafter, retreated from the church to became a lawyer. A top ranked figure in the Reagan administration's Justice Department in the mid 1980s, Giuliani returned home to became the U.S. Attorney for the Southern District of New York. Married to Donna Hanover, a local TV news anchorperson, Giuliani never passed up an opportunity to announce a blockbuster bust, even ones that resulted in no convictions. A liberal Democrat turned Republican, he ran for U.S. Senate in 2000 against Hillary Rodham Clinton. Pundits wondered whether a man described as "nasty" and the "dictator of New York" could beat the First Lady and her village of Democratic support. However, according to a New York observer, "One man's Hitler is another man's Abraham Lincoln."

RUDOLPH GIULIANI DOES THE DUMBEST THINGS

✪ In 1974, Giuliani the lawyer prosecuted Rep. Bertram T. Podell (D-New York) in a bribery trial. Rudy's questioning was so fierce that the fidgeting defendant poked out the lens of his eyeglasses, took a recess, then admitted he was guilty. After the incident, Giuliani switched from the Democratic Party to the Republican Party, claiming that the Democratic view of the world was "dangerous."

✪ White-collar-crime-busting Giuliani arrested three Wall Street investment bankers in dramatic fashion, confronting two of them at their offices and one at home. Rudy trumpeted his achievement, grabbing headlines as he proclaimed to have cracked a multi-million dollar insider trading ring. However, as the trial date approached, he decided he didn't have a case, and dropped the charges.

✪ Just as Giuliani stepped to the lectern to give his inaugural address as mayor of New York City, his seven-year-old son, Andrew, appeared on stage. While his daddy spoke, Andrew made faces, knocked over a pitcher of water, and repeated his father's line, "It should be so and it will be so." When his dad stepped away from the lectern to express appreciation to his predecessor, young Andrew rushed to the open mike and shouted, "Me, too!" Afterward, Giuliani said of the speech, "It was great," and claimed that his son had helped him write it.

✪ Mayor Giuliani ejected Palestinian leader Yasser Arafat from a concert at the United Nations. Arafat claimed that Giuliani's chief of staff shouted, "Go to Hell! Go away!" Shortly thereafter, Arafat won the Nobel Peace Prize, while Rudy defiantly declared, "I would not invite Yasser Arafat to anything, anywhere, anytime, anyplace."

Rudy Giuliani did not serve elephant dung to the folks at the Bowery Mission on Thanksgiving in 1996. In fact, he hated elephant dung, especially if it was glued to a painting of the Virgin Mary. When the Brooklyn Museum of Art featured a dung encrusted Virgin in a 1999 exhibition, Giuliani cut off city funds to the museum. The result of Giuliani's outrage? The exhibition was a blockbuster success.

(Courtesy of Archive Photos/Stefania Zamparelli)

★ In 1997, Giuliani was on the campaign trail for reelection as mayor. Unfortunately, his wife Donna Hanover didn't help much. She dropped Giuliani from her name, refused to campaign for him, wouldn't appear with him at his victory party, and declined to say if she had voted for him. Most people suspected marital difficulties, but Donna insisted she was focusing on her own career. And what was her profession? Acting and appearing on the Food Network.

★ Rudolph was at least as good an actor as his non-supportive spouse. For the finale of a 1997 $400-a-plate, black-tie dinner, Giuliani stepped out on-stage in a blond wig, heavy makeup, and a bosomy gown and proceeded to impersonate Marilyn Monroe singing "Happy Birthday, Mr. President" to John F. Kennedy. Later in the fundraiser, Mayor Rudy claimed that his female alter ego was called "Rudia."

★ Giuliani later played himself on episodes of the TV shows *Guiding Light* and *Seinfeld*. In November 1997, he appeared as the guest host of TV's *Saturday Night Live*. In one skit about Thanksgiving, Rudy appeared as a hairy, big busted Italian grandmother in a floral dress, and cracked a joke about "master-basting." He also appeared as a Catholic school teacher and discussed hickeys, psychotropic drugs, and tongue kissing.

✪ In 1997, rumors surfaced that the mayor allegedly was having an affair with his communications director, Cristyne Lategano. Giuliani denied the gossip, but Lategano was forced out of her job, reportedly by Giuliani's wife. Rudy claimed that he had hired her because of her credentials as a Yankees fan.

✪ In June 1998, Giuliani approved construction of a $15.1 million bulletproof bunker to protect him and his staff in case of natural or manmade disasters. The command center was to be constructed across the street from the World Trade Center Twin Towers, the site of the worst terrorist attack in New York City history.

✪ Giuliani hosted his own radio talk show in New York City, but sometimes lost patience with the citizens of the Big Apple. For example, when a caller asked about New York City's ban on pet ferrets, the mayor snapped, "There is something deranged about you. You should go consult a psychologist or a psychiatrist with this excessive concern—how you are devoting your life to weasels."

✪ In April 1999, Giuliani declared that the New York City school system was "dysfunctional" and "should be blown up."

✪ When it became clear that Hillary Clinton would run in 2000 as the Democratic candidate for the Senate from New York, Giuliani toured the state to deride Hillary as a carpetbagger, since she was not really a resident of New York. But while he was in college, Rudy did not think that being a "carpetbagger" was such a bad thing. At that time, he was supporting Bobby Kennedy's bid for a Senate seat from New York, even though Kennedy didn't reside in the state. "The carpetbagger issue," Giuliani wrote, "is a truly ridiculous reason for not voting for a man in the year 1964." The future mayor even cited the case of Rufus King, the first senator from New York elected to the U.S. Senate in 1789, who lived in Massachusetts until his election.

Phil Gramm

FACTS OF LIFE

ORIGIN: Born William Philip Gramm, July 8, 1942, Fort Benning, Georgia.

FORMATIVE YEARS: University of Georgia, B.A. 1964; Ph.D. 1967.

FAMILY PLANNING: Married Sharon (high school teacher), 1963; divorced, c. 1969; married Wendy Lee (professor), 1970.

SELECTED ELECTION SCORECARD: 1976: lost, U.S. Senate, Texas. 1978–82: won, U.S. House of Representatives, 16th District, Texas. 1983: won, U.S. House of Representatives, 16th District, Texas (in a special election held after Gramm switched from the Democratic Party to the Republican Party). 1984–96: won, U.S. Senate, Texas. 1996: lost, U.S. president.

QUICKIE BIO

Phil Gramm was a hard-driving conservative who loved the free enterprise system so much that he never worked in the private sector. Born to an army sergeant who died young, the child Gramm flunked third, seventh, and ninth grades, but managed to get a doctorate in economics. Phil taught at Texas A&M University in the 1970s, until he got bitten by the political bug and won a seat in the House of Representatives as a Democrat. Gramm switched parties but managed to keep his Congressional seat, won a place in the Senate and set his sights for the White House in 1996. At a fundraising dinner to kick off his campaign, Texas governor George W. Bush reminded the crowd that a president had to have good looks and charisma. Bush turned his head toward Gramm and said, "You don't have that!" So true, so true . . .

PHIL GRAMM DOES
THE DUMBEST THINGS

★ As an economist, Gramm wrote a research paper on entrepreneurial whale hunters. He also delivered a lecture entitled "Government is the Enemy," while he took a government paycheck.

★ In 1973, Gramm's wife's sister's husband, a movie producer, showed Phil rushes of a film he was making called *Truck Stop Women*. Phil's former brother-in-law recalled that Gramm was "titillated because there was frontal nudity in it" and tried to invest in the film. *Truck Stop Women* did not need investors, but the film *Beauty Queens* did. The same relative recalled, "It was a sexploitation of beauty contests, how all the beauty queens are screwing the contest judges to win. We gave Phil the script to read and he loved it." Gramm got a colleague's wife to front for his financial support, however, since "he was contemplating a run for political office, and didn't want the investment in his name."

★ Mid-project, the director of *Beauty Queens* decided to shelve the film in favor of an X-rated satire of the Richard Nixon presidency, *White House Madness*. The picture was written by the founder of the Cockettes, a San Francisco group of female impersonators, and portrayed Watergate as Nixon's attempt to cover up a sexual relationship with his dog Checkers. Gramm had backed Nixon in the 1968 and 1972 presidential elections, and, according to his brother-in-law, was also an enthusiastic backer of the film.

"I'm with Ronald Reagan on that one. Whatever he said about it," Phil Gramm declared.
(Courtesy of Ron Sachs/Consolidated News Pictures/Archive Photos)

★ Sexy Phil often thought about voluptuous Italian movie star Sophia Loren. He described his 1989 budget reduction plan as "something between kissing Sophia Loren in the moonlight and kissing your maiden aunt in a nursing home." When asked in 1995 by TV talk-show maven Larry King if he would choose a woman to be his vice presidential running mate, he shot back, "Sophia Loren is not a citizen."

★ Gramm liked to prove he was tough. During a debate on Social Security, one critic said that Phil's proposals would be very hard on eighty-year-olds. "Most people don't have the luxury of living to be eighty years old," he snarled. "So it's hard for me to feel sorry for them."

★ When an elderly widow approached Gramm and said that his proposals to cut Social Security and Medicaid benefits would make it hard for her to remain financially independent, he suggested, "You haven't thought of a new husband, have you?"

★ After Phil began running for the Republican presidential nomination in 1995, his loyal wife Wendy tried to do her part by participating in the Cycle Across Maryland Tour. Most of the other entries rode bicycles, but Wendy decided to Rollerblade for 105 miles. She collapsed on the road and was hospitalized for heat exhaustion.

★ While Wendy was skating, her hubby was telling stories about their romance. Gramm said that he met her during his second year at Texas A&M when he interviewed her for a job in his department. Phil recalled that it was love at first sight, at least on his part. "In helping her on with her coat . . . I said to her, 'As a single member of the faculty, I'd be especially interested in your coming to Texas A&M.' She looked up at me and said, 'Yuck!' I went back into the room and told the interview committee, 'We are going to convince her to come to Texas A&M, and I am going to marry her.' " Wendy joined the faculty several months later. They wed just two months after that, but only after she twice rejected his marriage proposal.

★ Federal budget balancer Phil once bragged, "I'm carrying so much pork [home to Texas] I'm beginning to get trichinosis," and fought hard to have the superconducting supercollider built in Texas. The proposed atom smasher, which required forty-four miles of underground tunnel, was budgeted at a total cost of $3.9 billion, or $38,500 per square inch. When the project's budget ballooned to $11 billion in October 1993, Congress cut off funding, leaving behind a five-mile long, $2 billion tunnel in the Texas prairie. One man proposed buying the abandoned supercollider boondoggle to grow mushrooms.

★ In his 1996 race for Senate, Gramm defeated Democratic challenger Victor Morales, a high school civics teacher who lost much of his support when he called an Hispanic rival a "coconut."

★ Gramm's down home Texas routine sometimes baffled his fellow Republicans. When Phil proclaimed, "You can't eat corn if you ain't a pig." Rep. Sonny Bono (R-California) turned to his wife and asked, "What the hell does that mean?"

Warren G. Harding

All-American Presidential Bonus Chapter

FACTS OF LIFE (and Death)

ORIGIN: Born Warren Gamaliel Harding, November 2, 1865, Corsica, Ohio; died August 2, 1923, San Francisco, California. Official cause of death was a cerebral hemorrhage, though it was first announced as food poisoning from eating tainted crab meat.

FORMATIVE YEARS: Ohio Central College, Iberia, Ohio, graduated 1882.

FAMILY PLANNING: Married Florence "Flossie" Mabel Kling De Wolfe (piano teacher), July 8, 1891.

SELECTED ELECTION SCORECARD: 1910: lost, governor, Ohio. 1914: won, U.S. Senate, Ohio. 1920: won, U.S. president (died in 1923 while still in office).

QUICKIE BIO

I don't know much about Americanism," Warren Harding once declared, "but it's a damn good word with which to carry an election." As it turned out, President Harding didn't know much about anything—except womanizing, drinking, gambling, and helping out his corrupt friends. Described as "an amiable rake" who taught school, sold insurance, and won a newspaper business in a poker game, Harding became a successful small-town publisher. He served in the Ohio State Senate at the beginning of the twentieth century and later became Ohio's lieutenant governor. Warren might have remained out of the national scene and out of trouble if it hadn't been for his ambitious wife, Flossie, whom he affectionately referred to as "Boss." Although he campaigned for the U.S. presidency with the slogan "Get Back to Normalcy with Harding and [Calvin] Coolidge," Harding's administration was much more corrupt than normal. Warren got back at his wife's high ambitions by having numerous affairs, including passionate interludes in White House closets—close to the same spots where Bill Clinton indulged his cigars seventy years later. However, Harding was far dumber than Clinton. Not only did he have several liaisons while in public office, he was a compulsive letter writer who preserved all the details in passionate love letters which turned up years after his death. Harding died in office and was succeeded by Calvin Coolidge. "I think the American people want a solemn a** as a president," "Silent Cal" declared. "And I think I'll go along with them."

WARREN G. HARDING DOES THE DUMBEST THINGS

★ Florence Harding was a piano teacher, who got pregnant by an alcoholic boyfriend at age nineteen, whom she wed and then divorced. Three years after marrying Florence, Harding had an affair with Susan Hodder, his wife's childhood friend and next-door neighbor. Susan gave birth to Harding's love child, a girl, in Nebraska in 1895. Harding supported the youngster while she was growing up.

★ Rosa Cecilia Hoyle claimed to have given birth to Harding's only illegitimate son. When Augusta Cole got pregnant by the politician, Warren reportedly sent her to the Battle Creek Sanitarium to have an abortion. The Michigan-based facility was operated by Dr. John Harvey Kellogg, the inventor of corn flakes.

★ An unnamed woman from upstate New York was so upset when Warren didn't leave Florence and buy her a home in Big Moose, New York (in the Adirondack Mountains area north of Utica), that she committed suicide.

★ On a trip back to Ohio, Senator Harding and friends visited a farm. One of the group heard squealing out back, and went around the house to discover Warren and his buddies squirting teenage girls with a hose and laughing. One senator's wife sighed, "He took rash chances with his reputation."

⭐ Carrie Phillips, Florence Harding's closest adult friend, was Warren's most demanding mistress. Carrie and Warren made love everywhere from kitchen tables to the deck of an ocean liner. In 1914 after his election to the U.S. Senate, mistress Carrie demanded a car. Instead, Warren delayed and wrote her a poem. Nonetheless, Carrie still wanted the car. Warren finally bought her a Cadillac.

⭐ Harding wrote Carrie highly descriptive love notes. He would sign his letters "Jerry," a term he used to refer to his male organ.

⭐ Carrie began raising German shepherds during World War I and was rumored to be a German spy. When some young boys were embarrassed because the dogs mated in the yard, she declared, "I don't know why it embarrasses you. It's the kind of thing I do all the time."

⭐ In early 1920, Carrie Phillips demanded that Harding pay up or she would reveal his passionate letters. "I will pay you $5,000 per year, in March each year," Harding wrote back to her, "so long as I am in that public service." Harding then went to the Republican convention, accepted his party's nomination for president, but neglected to tell anyone about his arrangement with Carrie. The Republican National Committee sent Carrie and her husband to another continent under the pretense that he would study the "raw silk trade" and paid them $25,000 down and $2,000 a month.

⭐ One evening, President Harding visited a hideaway party house known as the Love Nest. As patrons threw bottles and glasses off of a table to clear it for dancing girls, they accidentally hit one of the girls on the head and knocked her unconscious. The woman later died. A drunk Harding was hustled out. The victim's brother tried to blackmail Harding but Warren's pals kept him quiet.

⭐ Harding had an affair with Grace Cross, a member of his Senate staff. After they had a fight, she made Harding crawl around in his pajamas in front of her friends.

⭐ Nan Britton was Harding's biggest indiscretion. As a teenager, she stopped by the Harding home often to talk with her idol, Warren, and sighed, "I was thrilled unspeakably under the touch of his hand."

⭐ When Nan turned twenty in 1917, she wrote Senator Harding asking if he remembered her and if he could help her get work. He said sure,

"Why Duchess, you know I have been out playing golf," President Harding reassured his suspicious wife. "Oh, no you haven't," the first lady snarled. "Where have you been? Out with a lot of hussies?" "Well," the president responded, "what of it?"
(Courtesy of Ohio Historical Society)

then took her to the bridal suite in the Manhattan Hotel. Fifty-one-year-old Harding kissed twenty-year-old Nan and exclaimed, "Oh, dearie, tell me it isn't hateful to you to have me kiss you!"

★ Nan and Warren made out in New York, and Indianapolis, and Chicago. But Nan was hard to get. When Harding suggested "love's sweetest intimacy," she was shocked. "[What] do you expect?" a frustrated Warren shrugged. "I'm a man, you know."

★ Finally, after registering at a hotel, Nan recalled, "I became Mr. Harding's bride—as he called me—on that day." Two house detectives broke in on the loving couple. They demanded to know Nan's name and age. Harding said she was twenty-one, but Nan corrected him and said she was twenty. When the detectives picked up Harding's hat, and noticed the name, they apologized and snuck him out of the hotel. The senator gave them a $20 bill. As they left in a taxi, the senator said to his girlfriend, "I thought I wouldn't get out of that [for] under $1000."

✪ Nan Britton claimed that Harding impregnated her at age twenty-two in his Senate cloakroom and that he was the father of her daughter. Warren moved Nan to Washington, and she took the name Miss Elizabeth Christian. The president introduced her to his buddies as his niece. Their daughter was named Elizabeth Ann Christian. Harding agreed to pay her $500 a month child support.

✪ "Somewhere there must be a book that tells all about it, where I could go to straighten it out in my mind," a confused Harding said about the issue of taxation. "But I don't know where the book is, and maybe I couldn't read it if I found it!"

✪ President Harding played poker twice a week with his Cabinet members. When he would run short of ready money, he would bet the White House china.

✪ Florence Harding, the president's wife, got her friend Charlie Forbes named head of the newly formed Veterans Bureau. Forbes reportedly took millions of dollars in kickbacks. When the Chief Executive found out, Harding choked Forbes in the Red Room of the White House, yelling, "You yellow rat! You double-crossing bastard!"

✪ So many of Harding's cabinet members had links to the oil business that reporters dubbed it the "Oil Cabinet." One of Harding's White House team, Albert Bacon Fall, took a bribe from an oil man in exchange for oil leases in California, then secretly leased the U.S. oil reserves in Wyoming, known as the Teapot Dome, to another oil man. As the Teapot Dome scandal unfolded, Fall took a fall. In 1931, he became the first former cabinet member ever to serve time in prison.

✪ After the Teapot Dome scandal, Harding's father told him, "Warren, it's a lucky thing you weren't born a girl, because you can't say no."

✪ Harding died under mysterious circumstances. After returning from a trip to Alaska, he fell ill. Florence's doctor, Charles E. Sawyer, diagnosed the illness as food poisoning from bad crabmeat and gave the president homeopathic remedies. A navy physician declared that the president suffered a heart attack. Most probably, Harding died of negligent homicide. The purgatives administered by his wife's doctor harmed his already weakened heart. About the incident, famed journalist William Allen White wrote, "How could the doctors diagnose an illness that was part terror, part shame, and part utter confusion!"

Jesse Helms

FACTS OF LIFE

ORIGIN: Born October 18, 1921, Monroe, North Carolina.

FORMATIVE YEARS: Wake Forest University, dropped out in 1940.

FAMILY PLANNING: Married Dorothy Jane Coble (reporter), October 31, 1942.

SELECTED ELECTION SCORECARD: 1972–96: won, U.S. Senate, North Carolina.

QUICKIE BIO

According to fundraising literature sent out by Sen. Jesse Helms's campaign, "Your tax dollars are being used to pay for grade school classes that teach our children that cannibalism, wife-swapping, and the murder of infants and the elderly are acceptable behavior." For twenty-five years, Jesse Helms served as a conservative Chicken Little, prophesying the downfall of American civilization as he continually insulted and confused leaders from around the world. Born to a policeman in the small town of Monroe, North Carolina, young Jesse was a tuba-playing drum major in high school, and was voted by his classmates "Most Obnoxious." As he grew up, Helms used his in-your-face behavior to tremendous advantage. He dropped out of college to become a newspaper reporter, then worked as a public relations man for the air force during World War II. Thereafter, Jesse joined WRAL-TV and made a name for himself as a commentator for the Tobacco Radio Network. Sort of a humorless Rush Limbaugh, Jesse liked to conclude his broadcasts with "the skies are getting cloudy" or "it is indeed later than we think." This politician first went to Washington as an administrative aide to Sen. Willis Smith (D-North Carolina) in the early 1950s, then returned triumphantly as a senator in 1972 and never left. Helms rose through the ranks of government to become chairman of the Senate Foreign Relations Committee (when the Republicans took control of Congress in 1996), one of the key people in the creation of U.S. foreign policy. All this from a man who once called the University of North Carolina the "University of Negroes and Communists."

JESSE HELMS DOES
THE DUMBEST THINGS

⭐ From 1962 to 1971, Helms contributed to a magazine called *The Citizen,* a racist journal from Mississippi that recommended pseudoscientific books such as *The Testing of Negro Intelligence.* Jesse called the tome "excellent and scholarly."

⭐ Jesse began his political career as a research assistant for conservative Sen. Willis Smith (D-North Carolina), who reached office in 1950 after a fierce race-baiting election campaign. One especially notorious campaign ad included a photo reportedly doctored to show the wife of Willis's opponent dancing with a black man. Helms denied it, but one of Helms's biographers was told by a former newspaper manager that Jesse, supposedly, personally doctored the shot.

⭐ Senator Helms supported the white apartheid government of South Africa. When black leader Nelson Mandela made his first state visit to the United States as president of South Africa and appeared at a reception to shake hands with U.S. senators, Jesse snubbed Mandela by turning his back and walking away.

⭐ Helms clashed with Sen. Carol Moseley-Braun (D-Illinois) over use of Confederate war symbols by the United Daughters of the Confederacy. "She screamed and hollered and cried about slavery," Helms sneered, "how terrible it made her feel to see the Confederate flag. I have been told she does not have a grandfather or a great-grandfather who was a slave, that she came from Trinidad or Jamaica or somewhere." Oops! Helms apparently didn't realize that blacks originally came to Trinidad and Jamaica as slaves.

⭐ In the Senate elevator with Sen. Moseley-Braun and Sen. Orrin Hatch (R-Utah), Helms turned to Hatch and reportedly said, "I'm going to make her cry. I'm going to sing 'Dixie' until she cries."

Jesse Helms believed in nutrition for kids. In 1981 he declared that tobacco was a valuable food product that could "feed a hungry world."
(Courtesy of Reuters/Donald Winslow/ Archive Photos)

⭐ "The war on poverty won't be won until we crack down on the lazy and the shiftless." Jesse declared. Later he observed, "The more we remove penalties for being a bum, the more bumism is going to blossom."

⭐ Helms tried to take over the CBS-TV network so that a conservative could "become Dan Rather's boss."

⭐ Jesse demanded that dictator Fidel Castro be removed from Cuba "in a vertical or horizontal position."

⭐ Helms, whose home state of North Carolina is a big producer of tobacco, liked to wear a hat that read "friends of tobacco."

⭐ Jesse opposed creation of the Martin Luther King Jr. national holiday. "You bet your life I don't like Martin Luther King because of his morals, and because he had people traveling with him who were really 'travelers' [communists]. This fellow out in California—I forget his name—he had been arrested twice and convicted on sodomy charges. He'd been with two sailors, one of them white, in the back of a car. That's the kind of folks King had around him." When a reporter pointed out that Helms's hero, J. Edgar Hoover, longtime head of the FBI, also had a lurid sexual history, Jesse sputtered, "Yeah. Well, uh, that's right."

✪ In 1984, the Helms campaign ran radio ads against his black opponent Jim Hunt that blared, "Yes! Black power is spreading like wildfire!"

✪ Jesse seemed to have a hard time telling people of color apart. As chairperson of the Senate Foreign Relations Committee, he discussed global political issues for an hour with Pakistani Prime Minister Benizir Bhutto. Just after completing his discussion, Helms introduced Bhutto as "the Prime Minister of India."

✪ Helms didn't think all blacks were bad. He claimed that his black maid was "a credit to her race." He fondly recalled an African-American golf caddy "whose gleaming white teeth broke open into a broad grin at the slightest provocation." And he praised "one of Raleigh's best known and most popular Negro men," a janitor named Dudley, although Jesse had to confess, "I never learned his last name."

✪ One night Helms appeared as a guest on TV's *Larry King Live*. "I know this might not be politically correct to say this," a caller to the talk program commented, "but I was just thinking you should get the Nobel Peace Prize for everything you've done to help keep down the n***ers." "Whoops," Helms responded. "Well, thank you, I think."

Local Loonies

Wacky, Way-Out
Bonus Chapter

DUMBEST QUOTES

"We do many things at the federal level that would be considered dishonest and illegal if done in the private sector."
(Donald Regan, Chief of Staff for Pres. Ronald Reagan)

"Capital punishment is our society's recognition of the sanctity of human life."
(Sen. Orrin Hatch [R-Utah])

"There are a lot of things we do that are irrelevant, but that's what the Senate is for."
(Sen. Alan Simpson [R-Wyoming])

"The present system may be flawed, but that's not to say that we in Congress can't make it worse."
(Rep. E. Clay Shaw [R-Florida])

LOCAL LOONIES PROFILE

Watch out! There are hundreds of thousands of them out there at this very minute—elected officials doing incredibly dumb things. You can find them in the sheriff's office, in the county courthouse, in city hall, in the courtrooms, in the great rotundas of the state capitol buildings, yes, even in the halls of the U. S. House of Representatives, the U. S. Senate, and the basement of the White House. Most of these men and women will make a name for themselves by doing one or two incredibly dumb things, and then disappear from public view. Although they may not have had the longevity of the Republicans listed separately in this book, their actions deserve recognition as among the dumbest on record. Below is an honor roll of some of those local loonies who deserve special recognition. Do you know of any local Republicans who might fit into this chapter? Do you have a published account to prove it? Then contact us on the Internet at *politicians@dumbest. com*. Your country will thank you, especially the Democrats.

LOCAL LOONIES
DO THE DUMBEST THINGS

REP. HENRY ALDRIDGE

⭐ During debate on whether to eliminate state-funded abortions for poor women, Aldridge (R-North Carolina House of Representatives) made remarks implying that incest and rape victims were sexually promiscuous individuals. A few days later, he tried to apologize, but, instead, wound up declaring that rape victims don't get pregnant. "The facts show that people who are raped—who are truly raped—the juices don't flow," the state senator declared, "the body functions don't work, and they don't get pregnant."

REGAN BROWN

⭐ During a campaign appearance, Texas Agricultural Commissioner Regan Brown (R-Texas) discussed a scourge that was sweeping Texas—a plague of fierce, biting fire ants. To prove that he was familiar with this particular insect problem, Regan called a press conference, pointed to an actual mound of fire ants, stuck his hand in the mound, and received thirty-two bites.

⭐ In a speech at an African-American college, Brown referred to Booker T. Washington as "that great black n***er." Regan later blamed a turkey sandwich for his politically incorrect (read, disastrous) statement, claiming that the sandwich had given him food poisoning and clouded his judgment.

REP. WES COOLEY

⭐ According to his ex-wife, Cooley (R-Oregon) once boasted that he was a U.S. government hit man who killed people with piano wire. He also claimed that he was a member of Phi Beta Kappa, the elite academic honor society. But during his 1994 Congressional campaign, he admitted that this was not true. He called it an "honest mistake," insisting that he'd confused Phi Beta Kappa with an honor society at the community college he had attended.

✪ At the unveiling of a Korean War Memorial, Cooley said that he had served as a demolition expert with an army Special Forces unit during the Korean War and had targeted North Korean positions. When challenged about his claim, Wes explained that his service records had been destroyed in a fire and that his commanding officer, Sgt. Major Clifford Poppy, was dead. Poppy, who was actually very much alive, said that Cooley lied about seeing action and had actually served as a clerk at Fort Bragg in North Carolina during the Korean conflict. Wes wrote to his wife at the time that he was working as a lifeguard, not a demolition expert. Cooley was arrested and sentenced for making false claims about his military service record in Oregon's official voter's pamphlet.

MAYOR D. A. COON

✪ Coon, the Republican mayor of Petersburg, Alaska, told a joke in 1991 about "barbecued black boys," then asked the crowd, "Is that racist?" Mayor Coon objected to Martin Luther King Jr. Day as an official holiday. "I've called it Martin Luther Coon Day all along and I think I have a right to do that because my last name is Coon," the mayor explained. "How does that grab you?"

SEN. CHARLES DAVIDSON

✪ Seeking the Republican nomination to Congress in 1996, Davidson (R-Alabama State Senate) wrote that God approved of slavery and that black slaves were grateful to masters who converted them to Christianity. His proof? A quote from the Bible's Book of Leviticus: "You may acquire male and female slaves from the pagan nations that are around you."

MAYOR DANIEL F. DEVLIN

✪ After losing his reelection campaign as the mayor of Darby, Pennsylvania, Daniel F. Devlin (R-Pennsylvania) got really depressed. He went to a local bank wearing a black baseball cap and sunglasses and declared, "This is a holdup. I have a bomb on me." After Mr. Devlin checked into a mental institution, one of his friends defended him by saying, "He's not that dumb."

REP. JAY DICKEY

✪ Dickey (R-Arkansas) went into a radio station to tape an interview in the summer of 1997, but he left his hound dog Romy in the car with the motor running and the air conditioner on to keep the dog cool. The hound dog managed to shift the van into drive and the vehicle slammed into the radio station building.

LARRY FLYNT

✪ *Hustler* magazine publisher Larry Flynt ran for president as a Republican in 1984, claiming that he belonged in the Republican party because he was "wealthy, white," and "pornographic."

REP. ENID GREEN [WARDHOLTZ]

✪ In June 1996, Joseph Wardholtz (R-Utah) declared that he would paint himself yellow "and sing like a canary" about his wife Enid's successful 1994 campaign for the House of Representatives from Utah. Joseph pleaded guilty to four fraud charges related to his wife's campaign, and admitted that he wrote $3 million worth of bad checks during the first three months of her term. Asked where the money went, the congresswoman's husband declared, "It went on her back, on her fingers, around her neck and on her walls. I didn't want to rent Henry Kissinger's house. That was her." His wife divorced him before her term expired, and dropped his last name.

MICHAEL GUBASH

✪ During his 1996 bid for a seat in the State Senate, Gubash (R-Minnesota) placed a combination political/personal ad in a singles magazine. "My name is Michael and I am running for state senator, Senate District 65," the ad read. "I am a god-fearing, moral, pro-life Republican. I am also seeking a faithful, devoted, obedient, God-fearing woman to be my wife, to share my life, and to bear my children." Gubash reportedly received no offers of marriage, and lost the election.

PRES. ULYSSES S. GRANT

✪ Grant (R-Ohio) was arrested for drunk driving—on his horse. He also smoked about twenty cigars a day and in 1862 presented a noted philanthropist with an exploding cigar. Later, while under treatment for cancer of the throat, the former U.S. president (1869–77) became addicted to cocaine.

Rep. Carl Gunter

✪ Gunter (R-Louisiana) had unique ideas about genetic engineering. "With incest," he speculated, "you could get super-smart kids."

Alexander M. Haig Jr.

✪ When President Reagan expressed concern about Cuba, his Secretary of State Alexander Haig said, "You just give me the word and I'll turn that f***ing island into a parking lot."

✪ Haig baffled Americans with a strange language that became known as Haigspeak. Examples include: "careful caution," "saddle myself with a statistical fence," "nuance-al differences," "epistemologicallywise," "definitizing an answer," and "I'll have to caveat my response, senator."

✪ After President Reagan was shot by John W. Hinckley Jr. in March 1981, Secretary of State Haig appeared at a press conference and declared, "As of now, I am in control here, in the White House, pending return of the vice president." When Secretary of Defense Caspar Weinberger reminded Haig that he was not legally in control of the White House, Alexander snarled, "Look, you better go home and read your Constitution, buddy. That's the way it is." Haig resigned from the Reagan administration shortly thereafter.

Rep. Martin Hoke

✪ Hoke (R-Ohio) gave the following reason for serving in the U.S. House of Representatives. "I could date [Congresswomen] Matia Cantwell or Blanche Lambert. They're hot!" Martin got overly enthusiastic for a female TV producer before delivering the Republican response to President Clinton's 1994 State of the Union Message. Hoke cupped his hands under his chest and observed, "She has the beeg breasts."

Gov. Forrest Hood "Fob" James Jr.

✪ At a meeting of the Alabama State Board of Education in 1995, James (R-Alabama) mocked the theory of evolution by walking around like a monkey with his shoulders hunched over and his arms hanging loosely. When Winton Blount, James's heavy-set opponent, criticized him during the 1998 Republican gubernatorial primary for his "walking across the stage like a monkey," Fob snapped, "Well, I'm a monkey that's in good shape. I'm not a fat monkey." James's wife Bobbie jumped into the fray, declaring Blount "a big, fat sissy."

★ James objected strongly when a judge ordered the Gideon society to stop throwing Bibles through the windows of school buses. The judge made his ruling after a student was injured by a hurtling Bible.

Rep. Richard Kelly

★ As a judge in Florida, Kelly (R-Florida) was impeached for harassing lawyers and fellow judges, and was later ordered to undergo psychiatric testing. After passing the exams, Kelly declared, "I'm the only member [of the House] certified to be sane."

★ During the Abscam scandal in the late 1970s, Kelly was captured on videotape purportedly taking money from an ex-convict dressed as an Arab sheik. On the tape, Kelly stuffed money into the coat and pants pockets of his suit, and asked, "Does it show?" In his defense, Kelly claimed he was playing along with the sheik, as part of his own investigation. He was convicted.

Pres. Abraham Lincoln

★ Lincoln (R-Illinois), like Nancy Reagan (Pres. Ronald Reagan's wife), was deeply interested in psychic phenomenon. He held seances at the White House, including one in which a piano was raised and moved around the room. Abe's wife, Mary Todd Lincoln, was a compulsive shopper who once bought 300 pairs of gloves in 120 days.

Byron "Low Tax" Looper

★ In his 1998 campaign against State Senator Tommy Burks (D-Tennessee), Byron Looper (R-Tennessee) took no chances that he would lose. A few weeks before election day, Looper, who had legally changed his middle name from Anthony to "Low Tax," was arrested for shooting and killing his opponent. According to one acquaintance, "His attitude was that we're all dumb and he's here to save us." When police came to arrest Looper, he offered them sodas. The widow of the man Looper killed won the race.

Ambassador Claire Booth Luce

★ Luce (R-Connecticut), a conservative congresswoman, reportedly once dropped LSD in Spain with a mystic philosopher and his male companion. She confronted nonexistence while having a bout of colitis, and spent her time hallucinating as she ran back and forth to the bathroom. The notes from her trip include the enigmatic command: "Capture green bug for future reference."

STATE REP. MIKE MARTIN

✪ Mike Martin (R-Texas) was known to his colleagues as "Little Ronnie" because of his admiration for Pres. Ronald Reagan. Martin was especially impressed by the publicity his hero received after John Hinkley's failed assassination attempt. In July 1981, Mike Martin was rushed to the hospital suffering from what he described as "six humongously large holes in my arm." Mike later claimed that he had been shot by members of a Satanic cult, the Guardians of the Underworld. Then he said that he had been shot by someone who wore a ski mask. Still later he insisted that he had not seen his attacker. As it turned out, Martin had hired his own cousin to shoot him. Why? Because he wanted to be just like Reagan. Martin's cousin actually exposed the faux assassination attempt. Why? Because Martin didn't pay him for his services.

✪ A month after the attack, Martin was arrested on an unrelated assault warrant. The arresting officers found Martin hiding in a stereo speaker cabinet.

✪ Texas officials later prosecuted Martin for lying to a grand jury about the shooting. Martin paid a fine and was released. The prosecuting attorney explained, "We can't keep politicians from having themselves shot." Martin later grew a beard and sued the cousin who shot him, claiming, "Regardless of the reason, that is against the law."

REP. JIM MEYER

✪ Meyer (R-Iowa) proposed legislation authorizing the federal government to pay one hundred dollars to any motorist who smashed into a deer. "This isn't a car problem," Meyer explained. "It's a deer problem." Colleagues considered the so-called "Bambi bill" "one of the dumbest pieces of legislation in history."

STATE SEN. DREW NIXON

✪ In October 1997, Nixon (R-Texas) solicited oral sex from an undercover police officer in Austin, Texas, and was arrested. After pleading guilty, Drew served his time on weekends and became the first Texan to serve time simultaneously in jail and in the state legislature.

SEN. BOIES PENROSE

✪ During an afternoon yacht party, Penrose (R-Pennsylvania) appeared on deck completely drunk and completely naked. A woman screamed and held her hands in front of her eyes. "Madame," Penrose lectured, "I grant that mine is not the form of Apollo, but it is too late for either of us to do anything about that. But if I present what to you are strange and unfamiliar phenomena, it is you who should be ashamed, not I." With that, the senator jumped into the water.

SEN. LARRY PRESSLER

✪ Pressler (R-South Dakota) once took a nap in a closet and slept through the beginning of a hearing. Later, he tried to leave a Commerce Committee meeting and instead walked into a closet. He was so embarrassed that he decided to wait until his colleagues left the room before coming out of the closet. Unfortunately, his considerate colleagues waited for him. And waited. And waited.

REP. STEVE STOCKMAN

✪ House Speaker Newt Gingrich appointed Stockman (R-Texas) to the House Gun Task Force to make recommendations on changing the gun laws. In 1995, Stockman wrote an article in *Guns & Ammo* magazine suggesting that the 1993 raid on the Branch Davidian compound near Waco, Texas, was staged by the Clinton Administration to convince Congress that it should ban assault weapons.

SEN. TED STEVENS

✪ Stevens (R-Alaska) complained about how badly the Democrats treated the Republicans and declared, "There's just enough Scotch in me to demand that I get my fair rights." Later, Ted had to explain that he meant Scotch blood, not Scotch whiskey.

REP. PATRICK SWINDALL

✪ Swindall (R-Georgia) was a minister and a politician. "I've spoken about a number of career opportunities," he observed after being convicted of perjury, "and one I've got to put into the blend is a prison ministry."

JOE TAYLOR

✪ In 1978, Taylor (R-Washington) ran for county sheriff. During a debate, Taylor was harshly criticizing Joe Kozar, his Democratic opponent, when he (Taylor) suffered a massive heart attack and fell to the ground. Kozar tried to help revive Taylor, but failed. "Death is death," Kozar observed. "It transcends politics."

James Watt

★ Watt served as Secretary of the Interior under Pres. Ronald Reagan. Watt, who described the environmental movement as "a left-wing cult dedicated to bringing down the type of government I believe in," believed so much in killing coyotes that he suggested First Lady Nancy Reagan wear a coyote coat.

★ "We have every kind of mixture you can have," Watt said, describing one of his advisory groups. "I have a black, I have a woman, two Jews, and a cripple." Soon after making the remark, Watt resigned.

Clayton Williams

★ Oil man, rancher, and communications executive Williams (R-Texas) invited reporters to his ranch as part of his bid to win the 1990 gubernatorial race in Texas. The down-home Republican started trading stories with the journalists. The topic of weather came up. Williams compared the weather to rape and chuckled, "If it's inevitable, just lay back and enjoy it." Inevitably, he lost the election.

John McCain

FACTS OF LIFE

ORIGIN: Born John Sidney McCain III, August 29, 1936, Panama Canal Zone.

FORMATIVE YEARS: U.S. Naval Academy, graduated 1958.

FAMILY PLANNING: Married Carol Shepp (divorced mother), 1965; divorced, 1980; married Cindy Hensley (heiress), 1980.

SELECTED ELECTION SCORECARD: 1982–84: won, U.S. House of Representatives, 1st District, Arizona. 1986–98: won, U.S. Senate, Arizona. 2000: potential candidate for U.S. president.

QUICKIE BIO

Punk," "Nasty," and "McNasty." Those were John McCain's nicknames when he was a hell-raising high-school student who visited juvenile court. Born into a navy family, McCain attended the U.S. Naval Academy just like Texas entrepreneur and politician Ross Perot. Unlike Perot, who did well at the Academy, McCain finished low in his class. John became a pilot and flew missions over Vietnam, where he was taken prisoner by the North Vietnamese in 1966. He spent over five years as a prisoner of war in Hanoi, thirty-one months of that time spent in solitary confinement. Later, he got into politics. Asked why, McCain claimed that his second wife, Cindy, liked to tell him his impulse toward public service was the result of "too many sharp blows to the head while I was in prison."

JOHN MCCAIN DOES THE DUMBEST THINGS

✪ In high school, McCain tried to pick up two older girls. When they turned him down, he reportedly yelled out, "Shove it up your a**!"

✪ At the Naval Academy, McCain was the unofficial head of a group of carousers known as the Bad Bunch. John acknowledged the he earned so many demerits by the end of his sophomore year that he was given enough extra marching duty to go from Annapolis to Baltimore and back seventeen times.

✪ John astounded his navy shipmates by his success with women. On his first cruise, he took shore leave in Rio de Janeiro, Argentina, and wound up having a liaison with a famous Brazilian fashion model. Soon after that, he had a fling with a tobacco heiress.

✪ When John attended flight school in Pensacola, Florida, his dating standards dropped a bit. He pursued school teachers and strippers.

✪ During his first race for the Senate, McCain jokingly referred to the Arizona retirement community "Leisure World" as "Seizure World." "The last election in 1984, ninety-nine percent of the people who lived there came out to vote," he yucked. "I think the other three percent were in intensive care."

✪ McCain was one of the "Keating Five," five senators who intervened with regulators on behalf of Charles Keating during the savings and loan scandal of the 1980s. John reportedly accepted $112,000 in contributions from Keating, including nine trips in Keating's airplanes and three Bahama vacations at Keating's expense. Keating was later convicted of fraud and racketeering in the collapse of the Lincoln Savings and Loan Bank.

✪ McCain was a fighter who liked to fight with his political colleagues. In 1985, Representative McCain launched into a swearing match with Rep. Marty Russo (D-Illinois) that escalated into a pushing match before the two were forcibly pulled apart. In 1993, Senator McCain mocked Sen. Edward Kennedy (D-Massachusetts) on the floor of the Senate and told Kennedy to "shut up." Kennedy told McCain to "shut up" and urged him to "act like a senator."

⭐ McCain had a very difficult time as a prisoner of war in Vietnam. Back in the United States, his wife Carol didn't have such a good time either. She was seriously injured in a car wreck, underwent twenty-three operations, and was a full four inches shorter when she was reunited with her husband. Soon after seeing his wife, John began socializing with other women, but denied rumors that he was going out with females under his command.

⭐ When the McCains' marriage finally broke up, some attributed it to the fact that the couple had suffered a long separation. Not Carol. "I attribute it more to John turning forty and wanting to be twenty-five again than I do to anything else."

⭐ McCain's second wife, Cindy, was the heiress to a beer fortune and supervised an international children's relief agency. Unfortunately, she was allegedly addicted to painkillers. Supposedly, instead of using the agency's charity funds to buy medication for needy children, Cindy used it to purchase painkillers for herself.

⭐ During his race for the Republican presidential nomination in 2000, McCain called movie star Leonardo DiCaprio "an androgynous wimp," then laughed and said, "There goes the thirteen-year-old vote." McCain later joked that he'd use "death threats" to get votes. "If you don't go out and vote for McCain," the veteran chuckled, "don't start your car for the next week."

⭐ Whenever a reporter mentioned McCain's temper in print, John flew into a rage. "I don't have a temper," he thundered regularly. "I just care passionately."

Joseph McCarthy

FACTS OF LIFE (and Death)

ORIGIN: Born Joseph Raymond McCarthy, November 14, 1908, Grand Chute Township, Wisconsin, died May 2, 1957, of liver ailments related to acute alcoholism.

FORMATIVE YEARS: Marquette University, LL.B. 1935.

FAMILY PLANNING: Married Jean Kerr (secretary), September 29, 1953.

SELECTED ELECTION SCORECARD: 1944: lost, U.S. Senate, Wisconsin. 1946–52: won, U.S. Senate, Wisconsin (died in office).

QUICKIE BIO

Pres. Dwight D. Eisenhower declared, "I just will not, I refuse—to get into the gutter with that guy." That guy was Sen. Joe McCarthy (R-Wisconsin), the Communist-baiting genius of "the big lie." The fifth of seven children born to a family in rural Wisconsin, Joe grew up poor before becoming a poor politician. He was a mediocre law student, and ran an unsuccessful law practice before winning election as a judge. His colleagues regarded his performance on the bench to be so bad that McCarthy, reportedly, was on the verge of impeachment before he left the courtroom to join the marines. He served with no particular distinction in World War II. Later, he ran for the Wisconsin State Senate and won. After being elected to the U.S. Senate, Joe saw his political career fading, until he "hit" upon the Communist subversion theme. Joe spent the next few years in a flurry of high-profile investigations, lugging around a briefcase bulging with files and a bottle of bourbon. However, when American TV audiences got an eyeful of the hateful senator during the Army-McCarthy hearings in 1954, the Senate censured him, and his power quickly evaporated. "Have you heard the latest?" President Eisenhower crowed, "McCarthyism is now McCarthywasm." And how many Communists did Joe actually catch during his reign of terror? Precisely 0.

JOSEPH McCARTHY DOES THE DUMBEST THINGS

★ McCarthy claimed that he was wounded in World War II and carried "ten pounds of shrapnel" in his leg. Actually, the injury to his limb was caused by a drunken fall during a shipboard party, not by shrapnel.

★ McCarthy bragged that he flew "30 dive-bombing missions" in the South Pacific. In reality, the only official such mission he was on was one to bomb an abandoned airfield. When he was airborne, however, Joe liked to play with the machine guns. One day, he fired off 47,000 rounds of ammo—not at the Japanese enemy, but at coconut trees. His buddies erected a huge sign which read, PROTECT OUR COCONUT TREES. SEND MCCARTHY BACK TO WISCONSIN. McCarthy later campaigned as a war hero and dubbed himself with the nickname "Tail Gunner Joe."

★ When it was time to undertake his bid for reelection to the Senate, McCarthy realized he had to come up with a gimmick if he was to succeed. So, in 1950, he stood before a group of Republicans, held aloft a piece of paper and declared, "I have here in my hand a list of 205 that were known to the Secretary of the State as being members of the Communist Party and who, nevertheless, are still working and shaping policy in the State Department." What did the crafty senator actually have in his hand? An old laundry list.

★ After winning his reelection to the Senate, Joe gained control of the Senate Permanent Subcommittee on Investigations, and grabbed headlines as he scrutinized possible Communists. In the purge, many entertainers were fired from their jobs and blacklisted simply because the congressman named them as targets of his investigating committee. The most ridiculous case? Madeline Lee, whose specialty was making baby noises on the radio, was targeted by McCarthy and blacklisted. Then, the long-running radio show *Amos 'n' Andy* was hit with protests, because one of the actresses on the program was Madeline Lee, a completely different person. Next, Camilia Ashland's show was blasted with protests. Why? Because Ms. Ashland *looked* like Ms. Lee. Finally, Madeleine Pierce was blacklisted. Why? Because she made baby noises on the radio that *sounded* like the noises made by Madeline Lee.

✪ One newspaper editor was summoned to McCarthy's office. The senator showed the newsman articles from a Communist paper denouncing the journalist. "Did you write that statement?" McCarthy asked. The editor thought he was joking. However, McCarthy persisted. Finally, the man solemnly denied under oath that he was the author of a statement denouncing himself. The editor left McCarthy's office and realized that in Joe's terrifying world "the existence of proof of innocence" became "damning evidence of guilt."

✪ McCarthy's supporters included famed conservative columnist/author William F. Buckley Jr. and political kingpin and former ambassador Joseph P. Kennedy. Buckley called McCarthy's smear campaign "a movement around which men of good will and stern morality can close ranks." Joe once played softball with the Kennedys but made four errors and had to sit out the rest of the game. Later he went out on Joe Kennedy's boat. "He almost drowned swimming behind it," Kennedy remembered, "but he never complained."

✪ McCarthy hired "Doc" Matthews in June 1953 to become executive director of his subcommittee's investigative staff. Matthews had just written an article entitled "Reds and Our Churches" which began, "The largest single group supporting the Communist apparatus in the United States today is composed of Protestant clergymen."

✪ In 1953, McCarthy employed Roy Cohn as chief counsel to the Senate Permanent Subcommittee on Investigations. In March 1953, Cohn and his close friend G. David Shine went to Europe to search for Communist literature housed in U.S. Information Agency overseas libraries. They visited twelve cities and six countries in seventeen days. At one point, journalists watched Shine chase Cohn around a hotel lobby, hitting him on the head with a newspaper. What was their most important discovery? That both the Russian and the American Information centers in Vienna carried books by Mark Twain.

✪ After Shine was drafted by the army, Cohn and McCarthy applied pressure to have him made an officer. When that failed, they arranged for Shine to take special leave from boot camp. At first, the army agreed to everything Cohn and McCarthy requested. However, when the army refused to allow David his special leave, Cohn threatened to "get the Army."

⭐ Joe's downfall began in April 1954 when the Army-McCarthy hearings began. It was the first Congressional investigation ever to be televised nationally. On camera, didactic Joe claimed that an African-American female clerk named Annie Lee Moss was a highly-placed Communist with access to confidential army information. But in her testimony, Moss confessed that she had never heard of the designations "confidential," "secret," or "top secret." When asked, "Did you ever hear of Karl Marx?" Miss Moss replied, "Who's that?" McCarthy fled the hearing.

⭐ After two months of testimony, everyone had had enough of dictatorial McCarthy. When a special committee of senators recommended censuring the overbearing McCarthy, the senator called the group "the unwitting handmaiden of the Communist Party." "I've been accused of many things during my long public career," said one big, athletic senator, "but this is the first time I've ever been accused of being anybody or anything's handmaiden!" Joe became only the sixth senator in U.S. history to be censured by the Senate.

⭐ After his political undoing, the senator climbed into the bottle. After one severe bender, he was taken to Bethesda Naval Hospital in Maryland supposedly for "a knee injury." Once in the facility, a furiously drunk McCarthy attacked the staff and broke a chair over one attendant's head. He was put into a padded cell and passed out. A few days later, "Tail Gunner Joe" passed away.

"Communists have the same right to vote as anyone else, don't they?" declared commie-hunting Joe McCarthy after Wisconsin communists helped elect him senator.
(Courtesy of Archive Photos/APA)

Richard M. Nixon

All-American Presidential Bonus Chapter

DUMBEST QUOTES

"All Jews are disloyal."

"When the president does it, it means it's not illegal."

"I have often thought that if there had been a good rap group around in those days, I would have chosen a career in music instead of politics."

"I would have made a good Pope."

"I got stoned in Caracas. I'll tell you one thing; it's a lot different from getting stoned at a Jaycee convention."

FACTS OF LIFE (and Death)

ORIGIN: Born Richard Milhous Nixon, January 9, 1913, Yorba Linda, California, died April 22, 1994, New York City, of complications from a stroke.

FORMATIVE YEARS: Whittier College, B.A. 1934; Duke University Law School, J.D. 1937.

FAMILY PLANNING: Married Thelma Catherine "Patricia" Ryan (school teacher), June 21, 1940.

SELECTED ELECTION SCORECARD: 1946–48: won, U.S. House of Representatives, 12th District, California. 1950: won, U.S. Senate, California. 1952–56: won, U.S. vice president under President Eisenhower. 1960: lost, U.S. president. 1962: lost, governor, California. 1968–72: won, U.S. president (resigned August 8, 1974, the first president ever to resign from office).

QUICKIE BIO

His former law partner called him an "equal opportunity hater." Alabama governor George Wallace dubbed him "a double-dealer, a two-timer." And Pres. Harry Truman described him as a "shifty-eyed, goddamn liar." Born to a poor Quaker family in Whittier, California, Nixon was named after Richard the Lionhearted (Richard I, King of England), but described his childhood self as "the biggest crybaby in [town]." As a ten-year-old, he signed letters to his mother, "Your good dog Richard." He worked as a rodeo barker and a chicken plucker, before beginning his political career at Whittier College where he stuck an outhouse on top of the school's annual bonfire. After serving in the navy and graduating from law school, Nixon began practicing law in Whittier, won election to Congress, and made his name chasing Communists with the House Un-American Activities Committee. A rabid poker player, Richard served as vice president to Dwight D. Eisenhower, lost a fiercely contested presidential election to John F. Kennedy in 1960, and finally gained the White House in 1968. A self-proclaimed "introvert in an extrovert profession," Nixon was described by H. R. Haldeman, his chief of staff, as "inexplicable, strange, hard to understand." In June 1972, four days after Nixon's operatives were caught breaking into the Watergate apartment/offices of the Democratic party in Washington, D.C., the president declared, "I don't think you're going to see a great, great uproar in this country about the Republican committee trying to bug the Democratic headquarters." Sorry, Dick . . .

RICHARD M. NIXON DOES
THE DUMBEST THINGS

✪ As a student at Duke University Law School, Richard Nixon once tried to break into the dean's office. He was caught and given a reprimand.

✪ The first night he met his wife-to-be Pat, he proposed to her. Her reaction, "I thought he was nuts or something."

✪ When reading the newspaper one day, the future president noticed a want ad seeking a "congressman candidate with no previous political experience." He answered the ad and won the election.

✪ Nixon's opponent in the 1950 race for his Congressional seat was for-mer actress Helen Gahagan Douglas, the wife of debonair movie star Melvyn Douglas. Dick passed out leaflets attacking Gahagan and describing her as "the pink lady" who was "pink all the way to her underwear." The smear literature was even printed on pink paper. Nixon claimed later, "I never said or implied that Helen Douglas was a Communist." She lost the election, but gave Nixon his nickname, "Tricky Dick."

✪ Before the 1952 presidential race, Vice Presidential Candidate Nixon was accused of having a slush fund that he used for private purposes. Nixon addressed the nation on TV, denied that he had taken the money, but admitted that he had received one gift. "You know what it was?" sweet-hearted Nixon informed the largest television audience in history thus far. "It was a little cocker spaniel dog, in a crate that had been sent all the way from Texas—black and white, spotted, and our little girl Tricia, the six-year-old, named it Checkers." Nixon and Eisenhower won the election.

✪ In 1958, Vice President Nixon visited Venezuela. A protester spat on the American, and was apprehended by the Secret Service. Nixon went up to the restrained protester, and kicked him in the shins. Nixon con-fessed, "Nothing I did all day made me feel any better."

✪ In 1958, the peripatetic vice president traveled to Hong Kong where he met twenty-something Marianna Liu, a tour guide and cocktail waitress. Later she moved to Nixon's hometown of Whittier, California. When a reporter inquired about her supposed relationship with the president, Liu snapped, "Are you trying to get me killed?"

✪ When asked at a press conference during the 1960 presidential cam-paign, "What major decisions of your administration has the vice pres-ident participated in?" Pres. Dwight D. Eisenhower responded, "If you give me a week, I might think of one." Ike often observed in private, "Dick just isn't presidential timber."

✪ For his presidential race against Congressman John F. Kennedy in 1960, Nixon's campaign produced the dumbest political buttons in his-tory. The buttons read: "You Can't Lick Our Dick."

✪ Nixon lost to Kennedy. Then in 1962 he was defeated in his bid for governor of California by Pat Brown. At the end of his concession speech, Richard told the press, "Just think how much you're going to be missing. You won't have Nixon to kick around anymore, because, gen-tlemen, this is my last press conference." Yeah, right.

The dumbest moment in White House history: December 21, 1970, 12:30 P.M., Richard Nixon confers with Elvis Presley. During his brief audience with the King, the president discussed the Beatles, communist brainwashing, hippies, and the drug culture. At the end of the meeting, the King hugged the president and presented him with a gold-plated .45 caliber pistol. The president gave the King a federal drug agent's badge. Elvis had been trying to diminish the drug problem for years, by eating as many pills as his physician would prescribe.
(Courtesy of Nixon Project, National Archives)

★ Nixon was elected president in 1968. Nixon's Chief Advisor on Domestic Affairs, John Ehrlichman, in referring to the Chief Executive's "Alice in Wonderland" outbursts and his "I am the president" instructions, recalled, "Nixon might say, 'I want all federal money cut off to MIT [Massachusetts Institute of Technology]. Do it now, do it today, there is no appeal.' So you would take a note of that and go out and do nothing."

★ Nixon did not enjoy pressing the flesh. At an airport a girl waved at him and shouted, "How is Smokey the Bear?" He smiled and turned away. But the girl insisted. His aide whispered in his ear, "Smokey the Bear, Washington National Zoo." Nixon turned to the girl, shook her hand, and said, "How do you do, Miss Bear."

★ Nixon liked to think of himself as a wine expert. At a state dinner in the White House, he ordered the waiter to hide the label of the $30 bottle of wine he was drinking. Why? His guests were drinking $6 wine.

★ Nixon was a football fanatic. As president, he sent plays to National Football League (NFL) coaches. Unfortunately, when a coach used one of the suggested strategies, his team lost thirteen yards.

✪ In 1970, while attending the funeral of French President Charles de Gaulle in Paris, Nixon told the crowd, "This is a great day for France!"

✪ When President Nixon visited the Great Wall of China with his Secretary of State, William Rogers, Richard observed, "I think you would have to agree, Mr. Secretary, that this is a great wall."

✪ In 1972, the U.S. military dropped thousands of "Democracy Kits" over North Vietnam. The packets included pen-and-pencil sets emblazoned with the signature of President Nixon.

✪ Also in 1972, Nixon took action against a domestic enemy. George McGovern, the Democratic nominee, was rapidly losing support, and Nixon's reelection as president seemed a sure thing. Still, it was not definite enough for Nixon. The president took the campaign out of the hands of the Republican National Committee and established CREEP, the Committee to Re-elect the President. On June 17, 1972, five CREEP employees were arrested for breaking into the Democratic National Committee headquarters at the Watergate apartment complex in Washington, D.C. "Look," the president explained to his staff, "breaking and entering and so forth, without accomplishing it, is not a hell of a lot of crime."

✪ Nixon won the presidential election in 1972. However, in May 1973, a seven-man Senate Select Committee on Presidential Campaign Activities began televised hearings about the Watergate break-in. As it turned out, Nixon had been organizing dumb stuff long before Watergate. In 1972, "Tricky Dick" ran a "dirty tricks" campaign to smear Democrats. What were some of the gambits? Supposedly sending out phony letters claiming that Sen. Henry Jackson (D-Washington) was homosexual, and that Sen. Hubert Humphrey (D-Minnesota) slept with hookers. The dumbest stunt was sending unordered pizzas to the campaign headquarters of Sen. Edmund Muskie (D-Maine).

✪ The dumb stuff extended back even earlier. One of the CREEP members, G. Gordon Liddy, was also a member of a team known as "the Plumbers Unit" because they operated out of a room in the basement of the Executive Office Building next to the White House. After researcher Daniel Ellsberg leaked the Pentagon papers, a top-secret study of the Vietnam War, to the media, Liddy was instructed by Nixon "to find out what Ellsberg was up to." How did Liddy do this? He burglarized the office of Ellsberg's psychiatrist. What did plumber Liddy find of interest? Nothing.

✪ Historian Theodore White described Liddy and the rest of the Watergate CREEP masterminds as "amateurs who were among the most stupid and criminal operators in electoral history." When H. R. Haldeman, Nixon's chief of staff, told the president about the Watergate break-in, and that Liddy had initiated the covert operation, the Chief Executive observed, "he must be a little nuts." Haldeman agreed, and reportedly described Liddy as "a little bit nutty." Another of Nixon's staff wondered about Liddy, "How did we ever turn a nut like that loose?"

★ Perhaps the dumbest thing that Nixon ever did was to have a voice-activated tape recording system installed in the White House in 1971. When investigators asked for the tapes, the president fought to keep them private, claiming "executive privilege." When he finally turned them over to investigators, it was discovered that one tape contained an eighteen-and-a-half-minute gap. Nixon's explanation? "Oh, that was just an accident that happened." Later investigation showed that the tape had been intentionally altered.

★ The most damaging evidence the tapes revealed was that Nixon ordered the FBI to stop their investigation of Watergate six days after the burglary. "I don't give a s*** what happens," the president fumed on tape. "I want you all to stonewall it, let them plead the Fifth Amendment, cover-up or anything else, if it'll save it, save the plan." Three days after the incriminating tapes were released, Nixon resigned.

★ As a result of the Watergate investigation, twenty-five individuals were indicted for a variety of charges, including conspiracy, burglary, eavesdropping, perjury, and obstruction of justice. Many of them went to jail. What happened to "Tricky Dick"? The House Judiciary Committee recommended three articles of impeachment: obstruction of justice, abuse of power, and defiance of Congressional subpoenas. The president resigned his office before he was impeached, was pardoned by the new Chief Executive, Gerald Ford, his former vice president, retired to California, collected his pension, and became a legend.

★ Moments before going on the air with TV talk show host David Frost in 1976, Nixon quipped, "Well, did you do any fornicating this weekend?"

★ In 1986, Nixon met rock superstar Bruce Springsteen and watched him sign autographs. "I notice that you sign your full name," Nixon told The Boss, "and it's such a very long name. When I was vice president, I remember going to see President Eisenhower while he was signing a stack of letters. He looked at me and said, 'Dick, you're lucky to have a short name.' "

★ Asked in April 1986 about the lessons of Watergate, a sadder, but wiser, Nixon said, "Just destroy all the tapes."

Bob Packwood

DUMBEST QUOTES

"I don't know how you decide ahead of time
what is going to be offensive. . . .
If you don't try, how do you know?"

FACTS OF LIFE

ORIGIN: Born Robert William Packwood, September 11, 1932, Portland, Oregon.

FORMATIVE YEARS: Willamette University, B.A. 1954; New York University Law School, LL.B. 1957.

FAMILY PLANNING: Married Georgia Ann Oberteuffer (secretary), November 25, 1964; divorced, 1990.

SELECTED ELECTION SCORECARD: 1968–95: won, U.S. Senate, Oregon (resigned October 1995).

QUICKIE BIO

I was such a shy guy growing up, I was a little afraid of women. I had no dates, and on the few occasions when I would try I was usually turned down. So I was hesitant to ask." Robert Packwood overcame his fear of women to become the most infamous womanizer to date ever to serve in the U.S. Senate. Born to a lawyer father who was prominent in Oregon politics, Packwood attended law school in New York City, and five years after graduating was elected to the Oregon State House of Representatives. He carried on in the tradition of his dad, who was described as a "flat out, abject drunk, and when he drank he became as mean as a cobra." Packwood enjoyed drinking after hours with his female aides, and gained a reputation as a skirt chaser. At parties, he reportedly leered at women, pinched them, etc. His lack of manners didn't hurt him politically, and he won an upset victory in 1968 to become the youngest member of the U.S. Senate. While defending women's rights, Senator Packwood displayed a passionate interest in the opposite sex. Whenever Senator Packwood came near a female, he started to pack wood. Bob finally resigned from office after a Senate ethics committee recommended that he be expelled for sexual misconduct, soliciting jobs for his ex-wife, and altering his diaries to obstruct a Congressional investigation. And who was the person who read all ten thousand words of the Packwood diary to determine which parts should be turned over to the Senate Ethics Committee and which parts were purely personal? Independent counsel Ken Starr, better known, later, for his investigation into President Clinton's private and business affairs.

BOB PACKWOOD DOES THE DUMBEST THINGS

✪ The dumbest thing Packwood ever did was keep a chronicle of his sexual indiscretions. Not only did Bob maintain a detailed diary, but he dictated it and had his secretary type out transcripts.

✪ Julie Meyers worked as an aide at Packwood's office in Portland, Oregon, after his first successful run for the Senate. Reportedly, Bob cornered her in the workplace, stood on her feet, and reached up her skirt, apparently intent on pulling down her panties. He stopped when she kicked him. A week later, as he stepped out to visit a Girl Scout meeting, Julie confronted him. "What was supposed to happen next?" she allegedly demanded. "Were we just going to lie down on the rug? Like animals in the zoo?" Packwood supposedly sighed, "I guess you're the type that wants a motel."

✪ Seven days after Portland's *Oregonian* newspaper published an article about the sorry incident, Packwood was interviewed by the sixty-four-year-old Washington correspondent of the paper. After the interview, Bob apparently tried to kiss the female reporter on the lips.

✪ In 1989, the Oregon politician purportedly tried a unique approach to seduce a twenty-two-year-old intern. He invited her into his office one evening and turned on a video about abortion. Then the senator pulled out a binder and started reciting dirty jokes to the young woman.

✪ After a staff party in 1989, Packwood had intimate relations with an aide on the floor of his Senate office. "She is a sexy thing," he recorded later in his diary. "Bright eyes and hair and had the ability to shift her hips . . . and she has the most stunning figure—big breasts." After making love, the two lay naked in the Senate office, sipping wine. "You have no idea the hold you have over people," the subordinate commented.

"I didn't use any gel on it at all," bragged Bob Packwood, referring to his hair.
(Courtesy of Archive Photos/Clement/Reuters)

"What is it?" the playboy senator asked. "Well," the aide answered, "I think it's your hair."

★ Packwood noted in his diaries that one of his female assistants had a "little body." When the aide complained to the senator that her boyfriend was cheating on her, Bob felt sorry for the woman, and believed, according to him, that is was his "Christian duty" to have sex with her six or seven times.

★ After the first accusations of sexual harassment were made, Packwood jumped to defend himself by agreeing to a TV interview with veteran media figure Barbara Walters. Not only did he tell Walters about "twenty-two staff members I'd made love to and probably seventy-five others I've had passionate relationships with," he carefully noted his confession in his diary.

★ After his divorce in 1990, Bob wanted to make sure that his ex-spouse was well taken care of, just as long as he wasn't paying for her. He approached lobbyists to give her part-time work so that he could lower his alimony payments and buy himself "a small, two-bedroom town-house." One lobbyist offered $37,500 for five years work and added, "If you're chairman of the Finance Committee I can probably double that."

★ What was an even bigger turn-on than sex for Packwood? Dusting! Bob's staff volunteered on a regular basis to clean his apartment. His hottest cleaning aide by far was Elaine. "When Elaine's here, boy . . . she uses furniture polish and dusts everything with Endust or whatever the stuff is. Pledge. Pledge furniture polish, I guess," the senator carefully noted in his diary. "And we Pine-Sol the floor."

★ When his diary was first subpoenaed by investigators, Packwood was concerned. Then he reconsidered. "Actually," Bob noted in his journal, "least of all damaging is probably the diary, because in it there would be nothing about a rejected suitor, only my successful exploits."

★ Upon being asked to turn his personal chronicle over to the Senate Ethics Committee, Packwood reportedly altered hundreds of diary entries. Not only did he break the law by doing this, but he also wrote about altering his diary—in his diary. "I'd like to change and have Cathy retype the diary so it shows something different," Bob wrote, "but it turns out the typeface is different and somebody can tell it."

Ron Paul

FACTS OF LIFE

ORIGIN: Born Ron E. Paul, August 20, 1935, Pittsburgh, Pennsylvania.

FORMATIVE YEARS: Gettysburg College, graduated 1957; Duke College of Medicine, M.D. 1961.

FAMILY PLANNING: Married Carol Wells, 1957.

SELECTED ELECTION SCORECARD: 1976: won, U.S. House of Representatives, 22nd District, Texas (in a special election). 1976: lost, U.S. House of Representatives, 22nd District, Texas (in the general election). 1978–82: won, U.S. House of Representatives, 22nd District, Texas. 1984: lost, U.S. Senate, Texas. 1988: lost, U.S. president (as a Libertarian). 1996–98: won, U.S. House of Representatives, 14th District, Texas (as a Republican).

QUICKIE BIO

If people want to live in a free society," Ron Paul once declared, "they must have gold as money." The Pittsburgh-born gynecologist and obstetrician acquired his unusual monetary beliefs while serving in the air force. Once he mustered out, he sought an environment in which his ultra-conservative eccentricities could blossom unfettered. In other words, he moved to Texas where, over time, he delivered 8,000 babies and entered politics. Elected three times to the U.S. Congress, Paul ran for president in 1988 as a Libertarian. "Are you sick of being chiseled, cheated, and conned by the politicians of both major parties?" Paul the Libertarian asked the voting public. "Are you tired of having your life run and your pocket picked by Washington, D.C.?"

Ron was not too sick and tired of politics as usual to rejoin the Republican Party and win back a seat in Congress in 1996. "The whole system we have today is built on fraud," insisted Paul, sounding like a 1960s student radical. Rep. Dick Armey (R-Texas) bragged, "We love him," but another Texas Republican leader sighed, "He's either an idiot or a genius." All in favor of idiot say, "Aye."

RON PAUL DOES THE DUMBEST THINGS

⭐ When Paul first entered Congress, he would not give his Social Security number to House officials. He claimed that providing the information was an encroachment on his freedom.

⭐ Ron criticized federal flood insurance, even when his Texas district was battered by raging waters and received huge amounts of federal flood insurance payments.

⭐ When Paul's constituents asked him to push forward a particular federal engineering project for the district, he claimed that he supported it, but referred to it as a boondoggle. The mayor of a town in his district said he loved the guy, but wished he was someone else's congressman.

⭐ Paul refused to make deals in Congress, and so achieved remarkably little results in his tenure there. The one thing he did achieve was the creation of a commission to study the role of gold in the domestic and international monetary system. Looking back on his record in office, Ron sighed, "In one way, I've accomplished a whole lot. In another way, I've accomplished absolutely nothing."

⭐ After he resigned from Congress, a woman came into Paul's medical practice office and asked for an appointment. The nurse said he wasn't there. "Well, where is he?" she asked. "He's running for president," the nurse replied. "President? President of what?" the patient asked. "You know, president of the United States." "What? You're joking!" the woman laughed. "My gynecologist is running for president."

⭐ While campaigning for president on the Libertarian ticket in 1988, Paul advocated that states should secede from the United States. "The right of secession should be ingrained in a free society," Ron wrote. "With disintegration of the Soviet Union, we too should consider it."

⭐ Libertarian Paul claimed that he would abolish every government function that could be performed by the private sector. When asked how, he said, "I would just do it."

✪ Ron advocated ending all drug laws and claimed that civil rights leader Jesse Jackson was dangerous. "He would use the army to invade personal property to find out if anyone was smoking a joint."

✪ Politician Paul later changed his tune. Instead of calling for the abolition of all drug laws, he claimed that he supported drug laws *if* they were enforced by the states.

✪ Libertarian Paul also advocated abolishing the Federal Reserve system, the Federal Bureau of Investigation, and the Fish and Wildlife Service, and legalizing prostitution. He claimed that he would lift every tariff on U.S. imports and shut down all foreign and domestic subsidies, and declared, "Aliens would be a great service to us because you'd create millions and millions of extra jobs and everybody in Texas would have an alien working for them." According to columnist James Kilpatrick, "In the conventional wisdom, what one says is that Dr. Paul is nuts."

✪ In 1992, Ron described the distinguished African-American politician and educator Rep. Barbara Jordan (D-Texas) as "a fraud" and wrote that "everything from her imitation British accent to her supposed expertise in law, to her distinguished career in public service is made up." After Jordan's death in January 1996, Paul called her "the archetypal half-educated victimologist, yet her race and sex protected her from criticism."

✪ "I think we can safely assume that 95 percent of the black males in that city [Washington, D.C.] are semi-criminal or entirely criminal," Paul wrote in 1992. In the same article, he claimed that "opinion polls consistently show that only about 5 percent of blacks have sensible political opinions."

✪ When Ron returned to Congress, once again, now, as a Republican, the former Libertarian became known as "Dr. No." In 1997, he voted against the Drug-Free Communities Act. How did the vote tally up? For: 420, Opposed: 1. During the 105th Congress, Paul was the lone "no" on twenty-seven votes.

✪ Ron claimed that the best thing about being a member of the U.S. House of Representatives was the annual Congressional baseball game.

✪ Paul claimed that he lived in fear of being "bombed by the federal government at another Waco." He recommended that Americans become citizens of Peru. "Peru recently announced that it will sell its citizenship to foreigners for $25,000," Ron told his newsletter subscribers. "If you're interested, drop me a note and include your telephone number, and I'll get you some interesting information."

Dan Quayle

"I love California. I practically grew up in Phoenix."

"I am not the problem. I am a Republican."

"It isn't pollution that's harming our environment.
It's the impurities in our air and water
that are doing it."

"If we don't succeed, we run the risk of failure."

"I have made good judgments in the past.
I have made good judgments in the future."

"Desert Storm was a stirring victory for the forces
of aggression and lawlessness."

"We are ready for any unforeseen event
that may or may not occur."

"I was recently on a tour of Latin America, and the
only regret I have was that I didn't study Latin harder
in school so I could converse with those people."

"For NASA, space is still a high priority."

"Mars is essentially in the same orbit. . . . Mars is
somewhat the same distance from the Sun,
which is very important. We have seen pictures
where there are canals, we believe, and water.
If there is water, that means there is oxygen.
If oxygen, that means we can breathe."

"A low voter turnout is an indication of
fewer people going to the polls."

"The future will be better tomorrow."

FACTS OF LIFE

ORIGIN: Born James Danforth Quayle, February 4, 1947, Indianapolis, Indiana.

FORMATIVE YEARS: DePauw University, B.A. 1969; Indiana University-Indianapolis Law School, J.D. 1974.

FAMILY PLANNING: Married Marilyn Tucker (law school student), 1972.

SELECTED ELECTION SCORECARD: 1976–78: won, U.S. House of Representatives, 6th District, Indiana. 1980–86: won, U.S. senator, Indiana. 1988: won, U.S. vice president, under Pres. George Bush. 1992: lost, U.S. vice president, under Pres. George Bush.

QUICKIE BIO

Dan Quayle once declared, "I stand by all the mis-statements." Man, there were a lot of them! Quayle wasn't born in a log cabin, but his dad's family did run the company that owned Lincoln Logs, as well as several newspapers in Indiana. Newspapers? Quayle? Unfortunately, Dan did not inherit a rapier-like wit. He attended college, but reportedly flunked the exam in his major, Political Science, the first time he took it. He went to law school, then went to work for his dad, who admitted that his son didn't "have the greatest smarts in the world." When Dan told his dad he was going to run for Congress in 1976, his parent said, "Go ahead, you won't win." However, Dan did win, won a Senate seat afterward, and then became vice president under George Bush. Reportedly, the running joke in Congress was, "The Secret Service is under orders that if Bush is shot, to shoot Quayle." Although he was without doubt the least swift speaker ever to serve as vice president, every once in awhile Dan said something smart. For example: "People that are really very weird can get into sensitive positions and have a tremendous impact on history."

DAN QUAYLE DOES
THE DUMBEST THINGS

★ In June 1992, Quayle was visiting a Trenton, New Jersey, elementary school and decided to emcee a spelling bee. He watched as a sixth grader spelled out "potato" on the blackboard. "That's not right," Quayle said, "what did you leave off? You need to put an 'e' on the end of it." "I knew he was wrong," the sixth grader sighed, "but since he's the vice president, I went and put an 'e' on and he said, 'That's right, now go and sit down.'" Later, this same sixth grader led the pledge of allegiance at the

> "Republicans understand the importance of bondage between a parent and child," declared Dan Quayle. Quayle also observed, "The Holocaust was an obscene period in our nation's history. I mean in this century's history. But we all lived in this century. I didn't live in this century."
> (Courtesy of the White House)

1992 Democratic National Convention and then was hired as a spokesperson for a company that made a computer spelling program.

✪ "Quite frankly," Dan declared, "teachers are the only profession that teach our children."

✪ When George Bush picked Quayle as his second in command, Quayle jumped around on the convention stage like a pogo dancer, grabbed Bush by the shoulder, and yelled, "Let's go get 'em! All right? You got it?"

✪ In August 1988, in Quayle's first appearance with presidential candidate George Bush, Dan explained why he vociferously supported the Vietnam War, but avoided the draft by joining the National Guard. "I didn't know in 1969 that I would be in this room today, I'll confess."

✪ "Hawaii has always been a very pivotal role in the Pacific," observed Vice President Dan Quayle on a visit there in 1989. "It is in the Pacific. It is a part of the United States that is an island that is right here."

✪ On a trip to Chile in 1990, Quayle lifted up a doll and an erection popped out—of the doll. Dan showed it to his wife and said, "I could take this home, Marilyn, this is something teenage boys might find of interest." "Dan," his wife insisted, "you're not getting that."

⭐ The former vice president was never involved in any sex scandals. According to his spouse, "Anyone who knows Dan Quayle knows he would rather play golf than have sex any day."

⭐ Dan Quayle served eight years on the Senate Armed Services Committee and bragged that he helped get cruise missiles "more accurate so that we can have precise precision."

⭐ In 1989, the vice president addressed the United Negro College Fund whose slogan was "A mind is a terrible thing to waste." Quayle looked out over the audience and said, "What a waste it is to lose one's mind. Or not to have a mind is being very wasteful. How true that is."

⭐ During the 1999 race for the Republican nomination for president, Dan's wife Marilyn called George W. Bush a "party frat-boy type." Yes, he was. Just like Dan. In fact, George W. belonged to the same fraternity as Dan Quayle: Delta Kappa Epsilon.

Ronald Reagan

All-American Presidential Bonus Chapter

DUMBEST QUOTES

"Even though there may be some misguided critics of what we're trying to do, I think we're on the wrong path."

"The system is still where it was with regard to the . . . uh . . . the . . . uh . . . the . . . uh . . . the . . . uh . . . progressivity."

"Nuclear war would be the greatest tragedy, I think, ever experienced by mankind in the history of mankind."

"The problem is—the deficit is—or should I say—wait a minute, the spending, or gross national product, forgive me—the spending is roughly 23 to 24 percent. So that it is in—it's what is increasing, while the revenues are staying proportionately the same and what would be the proper amount they should, that we should be taking from the private sector."

"Has anyone stopped to consider that the best way to balance the federal budget is not by taxing people into the poorhouse and it's not by cutting spending to the bone, but by all of us simply trying to live up to the Ten Commandments and the Golden Rule?"

FACTS OF LIFE

ORIGIN: Born Ronald Wilson Reagan, February 6, 1911, Tampico, Illinois.

FORMATIVE YEARS: Eureka College, B.A. 1932.

FAMILY PLANNING: Married Jane Wyman (actress), January 24, 1940; divorced, 1948; married Nancy Davis (Anne Frances Robbins) (actress), March 24, 1952.

SELECTED ELECTION SCORECARD: 1966–70: won, governor, California. 1968: lost, U.S. president. 1976: lost, U.S. president. 1980–84: won, U.S. president.

QUICKIE BIO

Described by his authorized biographer as "an apparent airhead" endowed with "encyclopedic ignorance," Ronald Reagan observed, "You'd be surprised how much [being] a good actor pays off." The star of fifty-four feature films, Ronald Reagan got into politics as an actor, and acted his way through his political career. After Ronald was born in a rented apartment above a bakery, his father said, "For such a little bit of a fat Dutchman, he makes a hell of a lot of noise." "Dutch" Reagan started his career as a sportscaster in the 1930s before heading to Hollywood where he became a contract player for a major Hollywood studio and starred in his first film in 1937. In his post World War II years, he was elected president of the Screen Actors Guild for several consecutive terms, while serving as an FBI informant. In the 1950s he became a corporate spokesperson for General Electric. In 1962, the self-described "near hopeless hemophiliac liberal" union leader became a conservative Republican, served as governor of California, and was finally elected, in 1980, as the oldest president of the United States. When Reagan left office in 1988, he had the highest approval rating of any president since Franklin Delano Roosevelt. Later it was revealed that Reagan suffered from Alzheimer's disease. And what was the title of the forgetfully good-natured president's autobiography? *Where's the Rest of Me?*

RONALD REAGAN DOES
THE DUMBEST THINGS

✪ Known as the "Errol Flynn of the Bs," Reagan costarred twice in movies with the actual Errol Flynn. (They also both made a cameo appearance on 1949's *It's a Great Feeling.*) The first time together on camera, Flynn loosened Reagan's saddle before a scene in *Santa Fe Trail* (1940). Ronald Reagan hopped on his horse, and fell on his butt. The second time they worked together—in *Desperate Journey* (1942)—Reagan delivered a line to Flynn. The swashbuckling star looked at the future president and scoffed, "Why don't you go f*** yourself?"

⭐ Ronald costarred with a chimp in *Bedtime for Bonzo* (1951). When asked to comment on the publicity stills for the screen comedy, the actor observed, "I'm the one with the watch."

⭐ Reagan's first wife was actress Jane Wyman. As grounds for divorce, Oscar-winning Wyman cited "continual arguments on his political views." She later claimed that her ex-spouse was "about as good in bed as he was on screen," in other words, a solid B.

⭐ After his divorce, Ronald lived the life of a swinging single. "I woke up one morning and I couldn't remember the name of the gal I was in bed with. I said, 'Hey, I gotta get a grip.' "

⭐ He tried to get a grip by proposing to actress Christine Larson, who turned him down. One of the last films Reagan ever made was *Hellcats of the Navy* (1957). His costar in the war story was an attractive actress named Nancy Davis. They dated, married, and had several children. Later, Reagan, the conservative, became the first divorced man ever to be elected president of the United States.

⭐ While running for governor of California in 1966, Ronald was asked what kind of governor he would become. His answer? "I don't know. I've never played a governor."

⭐ "We should declare war on North Vietnam," Reagan insisted in 1965. "We could pave the whole country and put parking strips on it and still be home by Christmas."

⭐ Ronald Reagan tried to be a good parent and attend his son Michael's graduation from boarding school. But when the boy approached his father at the event, papa Ron stuck out his hand and introduced himself. He didn't recognize his own child.

⭐ After he was elected president, Reagan was awakened by an assistant on the morning of his inauguration in January 1981. When the helper told Ronald that he was going to be sworn in that day, Reagan blinked his eyes and asked, "Does that mean I have to get up?"

⭐ While on a state visit to Brazil in 1982, President Reagan stood up and gave a toast to "the people of Bolivia." The Chief Executive later explained that he made the mistake because Bolivia was his next stop. Nice save, but it wasn't.

★ Later, Reagan talked about his 1982 tour through Latin America. "I didn't go down there with any plan for the Americas, or anything. I went down there to find out from them and their views. You'd be surprised. They're all individual countries."

★ "We did not—repeat, did not—trade weapons or anything else for hostages, nor will we," President Reagan declared in 1986. Actually, Reagan's White House secretly sold arms to Iran in exchange for assistance in getting hostages free from Lebanon. The Iranians were overcharged, and the money was given to the Contras, a revolutionary group in Nicaragua. Months before his staff made the weapons deal with Iran, Reagan referred to Iran as an "outlaw state run by the strangest collection of misfits, looney tunes, and squalid criminals since the advent of the Third Reich."

★ After the Iran-Contra scandal hit the headlines, Reagan declared, "A few months ago I told the American people I did not trade arms for hostages. My heart and my best intentions still tell me that's true, but the facts and the evidence tells me it is not."

★ "I could see where you could have an exchange of tactical [nuclear] weapons against troops in the field without it bringing either one of the major powers to pushing the button," declared Ronald Reagan. Reagan also told reporters gathered in the Oval Office that nuclear weapons "can't help but have an effect on the population as a whole."

★ Before a 1984 radio interview, President Reagan quipped, "My fellow Americans, I am pleased to tell you that I've signed legislation that will outlaw Russia forever. We begin bombing in five minutes." Oops! The microphone was turned on.

★ When people complained of oil derricks off the coast of Southern California, President Reagan in 1985 had an aesthetic suggestion. "We've got lots of freighters . . . up in mothballs. Why don't we bring down some and anchor them between the shore and the oil derrick? And then the people would see a ship, and they wouldn't find anything wrong with it."

★ "Ladies and Gentlemen," President Reagan said, welcoming Liberian leader Samuel K. Doe to the White House. "Chairman Moe of Liberia is our visitor here today, and we're very proud to have him."

★ At a White House reception for big-city mayors, the Chief Executive came up to an African-American attendee and said, "How are you, Mr.

Mayor? I'm glad to meet you. How are things in your city?" It was actually his only black Cabinet member, Samuel Pierce.

⭐ Reagan met with the Pope at the Vatican in June of 1982 and fell asleep. When his head nodded forward, he abruptly awoke.

⭐ In that same year, Ronald hosted a meeting of Arab leaders at the White House. "You know," the president said to the Lebanese foreign minister, "your nose looks just like Danny Thomas'."

⭐ At a debate with Democratic presidential candidate Walter Mondale in 1984, Reagan said that Armageddon could come "the day after tomorrow." First Lady Nancy Reagan gasped "Oh, no!"

⭐ In 1985, Reagan visited a Nazi graveyard in Bitburg, Germany, and declared that the German soldiers "were victims, just as surely as the victims in the concentration camps." His aide gasped, "Oh my God!"

⭐ Reagan was not only spacey, he launched the creation of the Star Wars missile defense system and liked to ponder the galaxies. "I've often wondered," the president mused, "what if all of us in the world discovered that we were threatened by an outer—a power from outer space, from another planet?"

⭐ On March 30, 1981, John Warnock Hinckley Jr. wounded President Reagan in an assassination attempt in Washington, D.C. Reagan's first words after getting shot were, "I forgot to duck."

⭐ After surgery to remove a bullet from his left lung, Reagan entertained himself by writing notes to the nurses like "Does Nancy know about us?" and "Send me to L.A., where I can see the air I'm breathing." Hinckley was found not guilty by reason of insanity.

⭐ Like Mrs. Warren G. Harding, Mrs. Ronald Reagan arranged her husband's daily schedule according to advice from an astrologer. When the press started asking the astrologer questions about the First Lady's schedule, Nancy reportedly phoned the astrologer and said, "Lie!"

⭐ In 1981, a woman sent President Reagan a letter complaining that she was having a hard time feeding her children with the reduced food stamps program. The letter wound up in Nancy Reagan's office. Supposedly, Nancy sent her back a recipe for a crabmeat and asparagus casserole.

⭐ When asked on Memorial Day in 1982 if he was going to visit the Vietnam Memorial, Reagan observed, "I can't tell unless somebody tells me. I never know where I'm going."

✪ "I don't think most people associate me with leeches or how to get them off," explained Nancy Reagan in 1987, a few days after she forced Donald Regan to resign as White House Chief of Staff. "But I know how to get them off. I'm an expert at it."

✪ Movie star Frank Sinatra believed Reagan was "a real right-wing John Birch Society nut—dumb and dangerous" and that Nancy was "a dope with fat ankles who could never make it as an actress." After the Reagans were elected to the White House, Ol' Blue Eyes sang for them and rumors persisted of a possible affair between the swinging crooner and Nancy.

THE WAY OUT, WACKY, MADE-UP WORLD OF RONALD REAGAN

✪ In November 1983, President Reagan told visiting Israelis that he had filmed the liberation of the concentration camps in Europe. Nope. Reagan never left the continental United States during World War II.

✪ According to Reagan, "Justice Oliver Wendell Holmes once said, 'Keep the government poor and remain free.' " No. Justice Holmes never said that.

✪ Per Ronald, "Some years ago, General Electric could produce light bulbs for half the price at which it was selling them. . . ." Nope. Never happened.

✪ When reporters asked Reagan what he had named his pet collie, Ronald answered, "Lassie." No. He hadn't. An aide later explained that the president couldn't remember his dog's real name so he just made something up.

✪ From the lips of Ronald: "Children have been born even down to the three month stage and have lived." No. Never has occurred.

✪ Said Reagan, "I'm no linguist, but I have been told that in the Russian language there isn't even a word for freedom." Incorrect. The word is *svoboda*.

✪ "There is today in the United States as much forest as there was when [George] Washington was at Valley Forge," stated Reagan. No. Not so.

PRESIDENT REAGAN'S WACKY FRIENDS

✪ Marine Corps officer Oliver L. North was assigned to White House duty with the National Security Council. Over the next few years in the 1980s, North reportedly ran a clandestine operation out of the White

First Lady Nancy Reagan declared that actor Mr. T was "a man I admire a lot."
(Courtesy of Ronald Reagan Library)

House in which he sold arms to Iranian terrorists, and transferred money to the Contra revolutionaries in Nicaragua. In defending his role in the Iran-Contra scandal, North declared, "[I] was provided with additional input that was radically different from the truth. I assisted in furthering that version."

⭐ Rob Owen was the courier for North's covert operation. His code name was TC for "The Courier." At one point, TC went to a Chinese market, and told a man, "Mooey sent me." The man rolled up his pant leg and handed TC ninety-five $100 bills. TC told the Iran-Contra Congressional investigative committee he loved Ollie "like a brother."

⭐ Fawn Hall sighed that Ollie was "every secretary's dream of a boss." She reportedly altered and shredded documents for her dream boss and smuggled papers out of the office in her boots and dress. She defended her actions by saying, "Sometimes, you have to go above the written law, I believe."

⭐ Hall later became a model and told TV interviewer Barbara Walters that her experiences with Ollie North "made me realize that probably I'm a lot deeper person than I thought I was." A few weeks later, Fawn ate a banana in a Washington subway and got a $10 fine.

★ In 1982, Dr. George Graham, a member of Reagan's Commission on Hunger declared, "As we look at the problems of our blacks, all we have to do is look at our sports page to see who are the best nourished in the country."

★ In March 1984, R. Leonard Vance, the Director of Health Standards at OSHA (Occupational Safety and Health Administration), told a House subcommittee investigating possible misconduct that he couldn't produce the reports they requested because his dog had thrown up on them.

★ Marianne Mele Hall, appointed as head of the Copyright Royalty Tribunal by President Reagan, coauthored a book in which she claimed that American blacks "insist on preserving their jungle freedoms." Later she insisted she was not the coauthor, but the editor and explained that as editor, "you don't need to understand . . . what you are reading."

FINAL THOUGHT

★ Reflecting on his White House years, Ronald Reagan observed, "You go to bed every night knowing that there are things you are not aware of."

Strom Thurmond

FACTS OF LIFE

ORIGIN: Born James Strom Thurmond, December 5, 1902 (dropped his first name in 1951), Edgefield, South Carolina.

FORMATIVE YEARS: Clemson University, B.S. 1923. Studied law privately and passed the South Carolina bar in 1930.

FAMILY PLANNING: Married Jean Crouch (secretary), November 7, 1947; widowed, 1960; married Nancy Moore (former Miss South Carolina), December 22, 1968; separated, 1991.

SELECTED ELECTION SCORECARD: 1946: won, governor, South Carolina. 1948: lost, U.S. president (as a States' Rights Democrat). 1950: lost, U.S. Senate, South Carolina. 1954–96: won, U.S. Senate, South Carolina.

"Inequality will exist as long as liberty exists," declared iron pumping Dixiecrat Strom Thurmond. "This is the choice Congress will have to make: Liberty or Equality."
(Courtesy of Reuters/Joe Marquette/Archive Photos)

QUICKIE BIO

I never thought Strom Thurmond actually hated black people," a black lawyer from South Carolina observed. "He just never really needed them." That is, until the mid-1960s when African-Americans began to vote in South Carolina, and Strom the Democratic "old seg" became Strom the Republican "Mr. Deliveryman." The oldest human being ever to serve in the U.S. Senate, Thurmond was born to a well-to-do political family in South Carolina. He first worked as a schoolteacher, then practiced law with his father, was elected to the South Carolina State Senate, and, during World War II, landed with the U.S. Army on D-Day in Europe. He was so opposed to President Truman's civil rights plans and desegregation of the army that in 1948 he split from the Democratic party and ran as a "Dixiecrat" for president. Thurmond carried four states, and went on to win a seat in the U.S. Senate, the only senator ever elected by a write-in campaign. In 1964, he became the first prominent Democratic politician to become a Republican. He also has become the Methuselah of American politics as he approaches his ninety-eighth birthday while still serving in the U.S. Senate. As one African-American supporter observed, "Strom Thurmond has never stabbed us in the back; he might stab us in the front, but never in the back."

STROM THURMOND DOES
THE DUMBEST THINGS

⭐ During his 1948 presidential campaign, Thurmond sent a letter to the governor of the Virgin Islands and invited him to be a guest at the governor's mansion. Oops! It turned out the governor of the Virgin Islands was black. "I would not have written him if I knew he was a Negro," Thurmond reasoned. "Of course, it would have been ridiculous to invite him."

⭐ In 1957, Thurmond denounced President Eisenhower's Civil Rights Bill as arming "the federal government with a vicious weapon to enforce race mixing." To delay its passage, Strom took the floor of the Senate and began talking at 8:45 P.M. on August 28. He didn't shut up until 9:12 P.M. the next day, after having droned on for over twenty-four hours, the longest filibuster in history. Luckily, Strom was wearing a diaper.

⭐ In 1963, a balding Thurmond began undergoing a series of hair transplants. In 1968, he told reporters that the secret of good health was blood circulation. He said that every morning he lay down on the floor and threw his feet over his head twenty five or thirty times. "Your brain has to be fed by fresh blood," Strom explained, "and if you don't exercise, your brain won't be supplied."

⭐ In 1947, the then forty-four-year-old governor proposed to his twenty-two-year-old secretary. How did he do it? By dictating a letter to her which described "the new duties which I desire you to undertake." When asked about their age difference, Strom replied, "I'd rather marry one twenty one years younger than twenty years older."

⭐ Before the wedding, Strom posed for *Life* magazine photographers, wearing only shorts and standing on his head. Why? The caption read, "Just to show he can."

⭐ In the 1950s, Thurmond insisted that the Civil Rights movement was tied to Communism. He called civil rights workers "agents of the Kremlin" and described black leaders as "the Red-tinted officials of the NAACP." After passage of the 1964 Civil Rights Bill, Thurmond declared, "This is a tragic day for America . . . this legislation will make a Czar of the president of the United States and a Rasputin of the Attorney General."

⭐ During the 1960s, Thurmond fought every civil rights measure he could find. When one of his committees tried to vote on one civil rights issue, Thurmond kept stepping out of the room to prevent a quorum. At one point, he passed the office of Sen. Ralph W. Yarborough (D-Texas) and said, "Tell you what, if you can take me in, then I'll go in there, but if I can keep you out, then you don't go in." The two senators started wrestling. Thurmond threw Yarborough to the floor and pinned him. Thurmond asked if Yarborough wanted to ask to be let up. The Texas senator refused. Another senator told them to knock it off before they had a heart attack. Eventually, they did.

✪ According to the Declaration of Independence, "We hold these truths to be self-evident, that all men are created equal. . . ." Strom Thurmond didn't agree. "The cry of equalitarians is not the American creed, but rather it is the creed of Marxism and the come-on of communism."

✪ In 1968, Thurmond married a woman who was forty-four years younger than he was. They had four children together.

✪ Ten years later, Thurmond ran a hard-fought race for the Senate. The secret to winning the campaign was to make the seventy-six-year-old candidate seem younger. To accomplish this, Strom's wife and kids traveled the state in a red-white-and-blue camper dubbed Strom Trek. Mrs. Thurmond explained, "Just as *Star Trek* on television brought good will throughout the galaxies, we hope to bring good will to the people of South Carolina." Strom himself displayed his youthful vigor by sliding down a pole at a fire station, three times, to make sure that reporters didn't miss their photo op.

✪ As Thurmond grew older, he needed the help of handlers to do his job as senator. For one committee hearing, Strom's assistants provided him with a list of questions to read. Thurmond read the queries, then kept reading the material, "If the first witness answers 'Yes,' then ask him . . ."

✪ The ninety-five-year-old Thurmond claimed that he was still a capable legislator, but he refused to wear a needed hearing aid, so he couldn't really follow any debate on the floor of the Senate.

J. C. Watts

FACTS OF LIFE

ORIGIN: Born Julius Caesar Watts, November 8, 1957, Eufaula, Oklahoma.

FORMATIVE YEARS: University of Oklahoma, B.A. 1981.

FAMILY PLANNING: Married Frankie Jones (childhood sweetheart).

SELECTED ELECTION SCORECARD: 1994–98: won, U.S. House of Representatives, 4th District, Oklahoma.

QUICKIE BIO

Watts began his career running on the football field, not for elected office. He first burst into the public eye as the quarterback for the University of Oklahoma's football squad, went on to play in the Canadian Football League, and returned to Oklahoma to get into the real estate business. In 1990 J. C. was elected to Oklahoma's Corporation Commission, the first Oklahoma African-American ever voted into statewide office. When his real estate business ran into trouble, Watts saw the light and, became a minister. A year later, the Republican Watts was elected to the U.S. House of Representatives, and became the only African-American Republican in Congress. Heralded as "the greatest communicator in the Republican Party," Watts was chosen as Chairman of the House Republican Conference in 1998, the fourth most powerful Republican position in the House. This Baptist minister was reportedly quite a lady's man in his day.

J.C. WATTS DOES
THE DUMBEST THINGS

⭐ Watts is not the only congressman to have a child out of wedlock, but he may be the only one to have two. Watt's two illegitimate offspring were conceived less than a month apart with different mothers during his last year of high school.

⭐ J. C. married the mother of one of the kids, and apparently abandoned the other child. When the mother, who was white, of this rejected child also ignored the baby, Watt's Uncle Wade adopted the child. Uncle Wade was a Democrat and former chairman of the NAACP. J. C. put out a press release in 1997 under the headline, "The Most Cherished Title—Dad."

⭐ Despite the fact that he supposedly abandoned one of his illegitimate children, J. C. was a major sponsor of Promise Keepers, a Christian organization that promotes responsible fatherhood.

⭐ Watts's father was also a Democrat. "I'm not like my boy," Dad explained. "I told him that voting for the Republican ticket is like a chicken voting for Colonel Sanders."

⭐ Darlene Watts, J. C.'s sister, went by the name "Chocolate" when she performed table dances at strip clubs for food stamps. After Chocolate went to prison for reportedly "engaging in an act of lewdness" and purported drug charges, J. C., who won the Christian Coalition's Friend of the Family Award, didn't visit her in jail. When he was criticized for abandoning his sibling, he finally did see her, but he also brought along a newspaper reporter and a photographer to publicize his family values.

⭐ J. C. Watts delivered the GOP response to Bill Clinton's 1997 State of the Union Address. Just before he offered his stirring rebuttal, Watts referred to African-American leaders as "race-hustling poverty pimps."

⭐ J. C. did a lot of "hustling" on his own. In the 1980s, two of his properties were foreclosed on, several of his other creditors went unsatisfied, and he was the target of lawsuits and other actions for alleged nonpayment of debts ranging from doctors' bills to a $25,000 investment loan.

⭐ In 1996, Watts refused to participate in a voluntary drug screening test offered to all members of the House. The reason? He claimed he didn't have the $30 lab fee. When challenged on the issue, he claimed it was a joke and that he had indeed been tested by another company.

⭐ In 1998, J. C. appeared on a TV special focusing on campaign finance reform. The documentary aired FBI wiretaps that seemingly showed Watts arranging to receive $1,500 in campaign contributions from three different firms regulated by the commission on which he was then sitting.

⭐ When Watts joined the House leadership in 1998, he was asked about his tax and campaign finance problems. The congressman issued a statement saying, "I regret that the demands of my transition into the office of chairman of the House Republican Conference do not allow me time to go over this ground again."

⭐ J. C. couldn't manage to keep his campaign promises. Watts ran on a term-limit platform in 1994, and said he would serve no more than three two-year terms. However, by the time of the 2000 campaign, Watts changed his mind. He declared that he would indeed leave Congress, but only if he was nominated as the Republican candidate for vice president.

"I've made dumb choices, and I'll make more," confessed J. C. Watts, who chose to become the only African-American Republican serving in the U. S. House of Representatives.
(Courtesy of Reuters/Rick T. Wilking/Archive Photos)

THE
THIRD-PARTY
POLITICIANS

Ross Perot

FACTS OF LIFE

ORIGIN: Born Henry Ray Perot (changed his name to Henry Ross at the age of twelve), June 27, 1930, Texarkana, Texas.

FORMATIVE YEARS: Attended Texarkana Community College for two years, in 1949 transferred to the U.S. Naval Academy, graduated 1953.

FAMILY PLANNING: Married Margot Birmingham (teacher), September 13, 1956.

SELECTED ELECTION SCORECARD: 1992: lost, U.S. president. 1996: lost, U.S. president.

QUICKIE BIO

Good guys don't necessarily finish first," billionaire Ross Perot declared, "and the world is not a fair place." Ross Perot was not a typical "good guy," and he did not finish first, at least in presidential elections. Born to a cotton broker in East Texas, young Perot earned spending money by breaking wild horses and delivering papers on horseback. Ambitious, competitive, and short, Perot became a naval officer, then quit to join IBM. Perot worked as a "salesman for IBM for five years, then formed his own company, Electronic Data Systems (EDS). Ross got the data processing contract for Medicare and Medicaid and was dubbed America's first "welfare billionaire." Described by journalists as an "elf with [a] banana nose and [a] putting green hairdo," Perot sold his company for $2.5 billion, and chose to run for president in

149

1992 as an Independent. Speaking bottom-linese in a high nasal voice, he wowed dissatisfied voters and won 19 percent of the votes for president, more than any third party candidate since 1912. He founded the Reform Party in 1996, and ran again for president in that year. However, by that time the public apparently had tired of his paranoia, his egotism, and his annoying voice. He received only 8 percent of the vote in 1996, and then was engulfed in a furious political battle for control of the party he had started, primarily against the new governor of Minnesota, Jesse "The Body" Ventura, who had won that office as a member of the Reform Party. Ross's well-touted motto was, "To know me is to love me."

ROSS PEROT DOES THE DUMBEST THINGS

✪ Ross met Margot Birmingham, his future wife, on a blind date in October 1952. Perot claimed, "It was love at first sight." Margot told a friend after the date, "Well, he was clean."

✪ As the only sailor who "didn't drink, didn't swear, and didn't mess around with women," Perot didn't think much of his mates in the U.S. Navy. He described them as "tattooed and drunk." He got an early discharge from the service. During his presidential campaign, he claimed that he left the seafaring service because his father was ill. At other times he claimed that he quit the navy because he objected to the seniority system. At one point, Perot insisted that it was all a misunderstanding as to the reason for his return to civilian life.

✪ In 1965, Ross hired a former IBM lobbyist to start EDS's first satellite office in Washington, D.C., and lobby for lucrative government contracts. Perot even lobbied for himself on occasion. In 1972, he met with Caspar Weinberger, Secretary of Health, Education, and Welfare, and demanded to be given the data processing contracts for Medicare. "I gave five million bucks to Nixon," Perot reportedly reasoned, "and I want that contract now!" He did not get the deal.

✪ During his first presidential bid, Ross changed his mind about lobbyists and claimed "they are really hurting this country."

✪ In the late 1960s Ross became a big booster of President Nixon. Supposedly, he promised $10 million to set up a pro-Nixon think tank and $50 million for media exposure, but never came forth with the funding. Special presidential counsel Charles Colson described it as "one of the most effective con jobs I ever saw in the White House."

★ After he launched a campaign to help the prisoners of war (POWs) and the missing in action (MIAs) in Vietnam, Ross claimed that the North Vietnamese had targeted him for assassination and had hired the Black Panthers to carry out the task. Perot insisted that one night he saw "five people coming across my front lawn with rifles." According to the Texan, his guard dog bit a "big piece out of the seat of one of the guys as he went over the fence. We thought we would be able to find that person, because if you take a tremendous hit to your seat, you bleed profusely." Perot's security guards claimed no knowledge of such an attack.

★ In 1981, Perot supported soldier of fortune "Bo" Gritz on a mission to Southeast Asia to search for POWs. "And I'm not interested in bones," Ross said. Gritz went to Southeast Asia, and claimed that he found POWs. His evidence? Bones. Unfortunately they were chicken bones. "I know a chicken bone," Gritz said in his own defense. "I eat a lot of Kentucky Fried Chicken."

★ In the late 1970s, Perot worked on an anti-drug task force for the state of Texas. He became convinced that he was going to be assassinated by the father of actor Woody Harrelson and assembled a security team to follow the elder Harrelson.

★ Ross hired former U.S. military counter-terrorist commandos to combat drugs smuggled into the United States and offered to buy a Caribbean island to set up an elaborate drug sting operation. In exchange, he wanted the exclusive contract to supply the island with gas and other services, "If I'm going to buy a damn island down there," he snarled, "I want my money back."

★ In December 1978, two top EDS executives were arrested in Iran. Perot called Henry Kissinger, Alexander Haig, and other high members of President Nixon's White House team to get help. After three days, he took matters into his own hands and created Operation Hotfoot (Help Our Two Friends Out of Tehran) to bust his employees out of prison. Tom Luce, his lawyer, called the plan "idiotic." Ross flew his crack team (the "Sunshine Boys") to Tehran, where they booked into the local Hyatt Hotel and spent their time studying the situation by watching TV. Meanwhile, rioting Iranian mobs stormed the prison and released all the prisoners. Perot's two freed employees hitchhiked to the Hyatt in Tehran. Ross later told reporters that the two executives had fled "through intense gunfire for about two miles on foot" and claimed that his squad was responsible for the escape.

"The planet is our home," the diminutive billionaire Ross Perot decreed. "If we destroy the planet, we've destroyed our home, so it is fundamentally important."
(Courtesy of Reuters/Peter Morgan/Archive Photos)

★ Ross paid best-selling novelist Ken Follett to write a book about the incident entitled *On Wings of Eagles* (1983), which was later made into a TV miniseries. Perot confessed that the action-packed, violent television offering deviated from the real story. "The biggest changes were: We didn't kill anybody . . ."

★ Ross later sold EDS to General Motors. Soon after, he began talking about "nuking" GM. The conglomerate offered Perot $700 million just to go away. "Why should I take this money?" the entrepreneur asked. "It would be morally wrong. I don't need it." Eventually, he accepted the funds.

★ During the 1992 presidential campaign, third-party candidate Perot promised to "get under the hood" of the national economy and said that the national debt was like a "crazy aunt in the basement." How to fix health care? "We will take it apart." He proposed a fifty cent a gallon gasoline tax, and promised to solve the deficit problem "without breaking a sweat." Mort Meyerson, his campaign manager, observed, "I could care less about politics. I rarely read a newspaper and I don't vote."

★ During a presidential debate with Democratic candidate Bill Clinton and Pres. George Bush, big-eared Perot piped up, "I'm all ears."

⭐ Perot dropped out of the presidential race in July 1992. Mort Meyerson was relieved that he "didn't have to continue going on the death march." But in late September 1992, Perot jumped back into the race. He claimed that he had quit because the Republicans were planning to disrupt his daughter's wedding.

⭐ As the election results came in, Perot and his wife had a party and danced to the Patsy Cline song "Crazy." Ross explained, "The devil made me do it."

Jesse Ventura

FACTS OF LIFE

ORIGIN: Born James George Janos, July 15, 1951, Minneapolis, Minnesota. (He later had his name legally changed to Jesse Ventura, and copyrighted it.)

FORMATIVE YEARS: Attended North Hennepin Community College for one year (1975), but dropped out to become a professional wrestler.

FAMILY PLANNING: Married Terry Larson (horse trainer), July 18, 1975.

SELECTED ELECTION SCORECARD: 1998: won, governor, Minnesota.

QUICKIE BIO

I'm not a Democrat," Jesse "The Body" Ventura declared, "I'm not a Republican." But when he announced, "I'm Czech!" his aunt corrected him: "You are not! You're Slovak!" A self-described "six-foot-four, 250-pound ex–Navy SEAL, pro wrestler, radio personality, and film actor," James Janos was born into a working class family in Minnesota. After serving in the military he joined a motorcycle gang and met his future wife while he was working as a "bouncer at a biker bar. Searching for a career path, Janos chose professional wrestling. He was a big fan of "Superstar" Billy Graham, so he dyed his hair blond and set out to be a bad guy. He started out as "Janos the Dirty," then

"Surfer" Jesse Ventura, then Jesse "The Body" Ventura. After he suffered pulmonary emboli in 1986, "The Body" became "The Mouth," as he quit wrestling to become a commentator and talk-radio host. He ran for mayor of his hometown, Brooklyn Park, Minnesota, after he got mad at developers who wanted to put in sidewalks and sewers. Later he got angry again, and decided to join the Reform Party and run for governor of Minnesota. He won the election, with the largest voter turnout in Minnesota's history. How did he do it? "The bottom line is that my opponents were boring." And what was one of the first political acts of the feather boa–wearing wrestler who once had referred to government as "cancer" and dubbed himself "Governor Klingon"? He tried to get his wife on the state payroll.

JESSE VENTURA DOES THE DUMBEST THINGS

✪ For years Ventura went for an annual "fishing" trip with his pals. They didn't do much fishing, but they did party in mobile homes with stereos and lots of fireworks and booze. Ventura explained, "It's roughing it. It's Minnesotan. It's the kind of trip where every waking moment you have a beer in your hand."

✪ As a wrestling bad guy, Jesse admitted, "It was usually my job to lose." However, he still claimed that this fact "in no way means it's fake."

✪ Jesse formed a rock band called Soldiers of Fortune, but admitted, "I really don't know whether or not we sucked. . . ."

✪ In his early days as a radio talk-show host, Jesse called one of his guests a "little commie," then, later apologized, and called the whole thing "stupid."

✪ Ventura criticized his gubernatorial opponents by saying, "Most of them wouldn't know crime if it came up and bit 'em on the a**." But when asked about what he would do about crime as governor, Ventura answered, "Nothing!"

✪ Ventura on the death penalty: "We don't have it here in Minnesota, thank God, and I won't advocate to get it." But he added, "There's another part of me that hears about these brutal mass murderers and thinks, Gee, maybe I'd like to walk over and pull the switch. Would that be a hands-on governor?"

✪ Jesse admitted that he did drugs beginning in high school, and justified his indulgence by explaining, "Back then, drugs were not a business, they were anti-establishment and provided escape." What is his answer to the drug problem today? "Let's regulate it!"

- When asked if he supported legalizing pot, Jesse straddled the issue. "Let's not talk about whether to make it legal or illegal, let's talk about the monetary potential."

- As a young man, Ventura enjoyed the company of hookers. "Incredible," he said, of Nevada brothels. "You go down the line, they each tell you their name, and you pick out the one you want. In those days it was cheap—ten to fifteen bucks." But not cheap enough for Jesse. He traded one prostitute a belt he had made from empty shell casings, for sexual favors *and* ten dollars. "I'm probably one of the only people in the world who's gone into a Nevada ranch and been paid. I used that ten dollars to go to another one."

- When he became governor he described prostitutes as a "social problem" and a "consensual crime." How best to fight it? According to Governor Ventura, "Volunteering."

- While he was a Navy SEAL, Jesse joined the anti–Vietnam War movement. Why? "I loved the braless thing. I'm very heterosexual. I'd see women out burning their bras and I'd go over with a lighter: 'Can I help?'"

"Organized religion is a sham and a crutch for weak-minded people who need strength in numbers," Jesse Ventura observed in *Playboy* magazine. He later claimed that being weak-minded was "not necessarily a detriment" and described his own wife as weak-minded because she went to church.
(Courtesy of Reuters/Eric Miller/ Archive Photos)

★ What did Ventura claim he would like to be reincarnated as? A size 38DD bra.

★ Jesse felt as strongly about gun control people as he felt about bras. "Gun control people don't know what they're talking about," he declared. "They're ignorant."

★ An avid conspiracy fan, Ventura liked to quote rock singer Jim Morrison and claimed that he wanted to retire to Hawaii and be a beach bum, saying, "It worked for Jim Morrison, didn't it?" Wrong: Jim Morrison of the Doors died of a heart attack in France.

★ The first lady of Minnesota, Terry Ventura, declared, "I'm not stupid. I went to Wendy Ward Charm School at Ward's when I was thirteen, excuse me. I know how to walk, how to get in and out of a car without showing the world everything."

BIBLIOGRAPHY

SELECTED PERIODICALS

Austin-American Statesman

Boston Globe

Current Biography

The Drudge Report

The Flynt Report

George

Globe

GQ

Houston Chronicle

Houston Press

Los Angeles Times

Mother Jones

National Enquirer

New York Times

The New Yorker

Newsweek

Official Congressional Directory

People

Sacramento Bee

Slate

Spy

Star

Talk

Time

USA Today

Vanity Fair

Wall Street Journal

Washington Post

BOOKS

Anthony, Carl Sferrazza. *Florence Harding: The First Lady, the Jazz Age, and the Death of America's Most Scandalous President.* New York: William Morrow, 1998.

Bakalar, Nick. *Republicanisms: The Bloopers and Bombast of the Grand Ole Party.* New York: John Wiley & Sons, 1996.

Barone, Michael, and Grant Ujifusa, with Richard E. Cohen. *The Almanac of American Politics 1998.* Washington, DC: National Journal, 1998.

Bauman, Robert. *The Gentleman from Maryland: The Conscience of a Gay Conservative.* New York: Arbor House, 1986.

Belsky, Gary. *On Second Thought: 365 of the Worst Promises, Predictions, and Pronouncements Ever Made!!!* Holbrook, MA: Adams Media Corp., 1999.

Boller, Paul F., Jr. *Congressional Anecdotes.* New York: Oxford University Press, 1991.

———. *Presidential Anecdotes.* New York: Penguin Books, 1986.

Bono, Sonny. *And the Beat Goes On.* New York: Pocket Books, 1992.

Brallier, Jess, and Sally Chabert. *Presidential Wit and Wisdom: Maxims, Mottoes, Sound Bites, Speeches, and Asides.* London: Penguin Books, 1996.

Bridges, Tyler. *The Rise of David Duke.* Jackson, MS: University Press of Mississippi, 1994.

Cannon, James. *Time and Chance: Gerald Ford's Appointment with History.* New York: HarperCollins, 1994.

Cawthorne, Nigel. *Sex Lives of the Presidents.* New York: St. Martin's Press, 1998.

Cockburn, Alexander, and Ken Silverstein. *Washington Babylon.* New York: Verso, 1996.

Cohodas, Nadine. *Strom Thurmond and the Politics of Southern Change.* New York: Simon & Schuster, 1993.

Cook, Fred J. *The Nightmare Decade: The Life and Times of Senator Joe McCarthy.* New York: Random House, 1971.

Coyne, John R. *The Impudent Snobs: Agnew vs. the Intellectual Establishment.* New Rochelle, NY: Arlington House, 1972.

Davis, Kenneth C. *Don't Know Much About History.* New York: Avon Books, 1990.

Dole, Bob, and Elizabeth Dole. *The Doles: Unlimited Partners.* New York: Simon & Schuster, 1988.

Duncan, Philip D., and Brian Nutting, ed. *CQ's Politics in America 2000: The 106th Congress.* Washington, DC: Congressional Quarterly, 1999.

Ford, Gerald R. *Humor and the Presidency.* New York: Arbor House, 1987.

Garment, Suzanne. *Scandal: The Culture of Mistrust in American Politics.* New York: Times Books, 1991.

Green, Mark, and Gail MacColl. *Reagan's Reign of Error.* New York: Pantheon Books, 1987.

Gregory, Leland H., III. *Great Government Goofs! Over 350 Loopy Laws, Hilarious Screwups, and Acts-idents of Congress.* New York: Dell, 1997.

————. *Presidential Indiscretions.* New York: Dell, 1999.

Hagood, Wesley O. *Presidential Sex: From the Founding Fathers to Bill Clinton.* New York: Citadel Press, 1995.

Hilton, Stanley G. *Senator for Sale: The Unauthorized Biography of Senator Robert Dole.* New York: St. Martin's Press, 1995.

Jackley, John L. *Below the Beltway: Money, Power and Sex in Bill Clinton's Washington.* New York: Regnery, 1996.

Kane, Joseph Nathan. *Presidential Fact Book.* New York: Random House, 1998.

Killian, Linda. *The Freshmen: Whatever Happened to the Republican Revolution?* Boulder, CO: Westview, 1998.

Kirchmeier, Mark. *Packwood: The Public and Private Life from Acclaim to Outrage.* New York: HarperCollins, 1995.

Kohn, George C. *Encyclopedia of American Scandal.* New York: Facts on File, 1989.

Kohut, John J. *Stupid Government Tricks.* New York: Plume, 1995.

Kohut, John J., and Roland Sweet. *Dumb, Dumber, Dumbest.* New York: Plume, 1996.

————. *More Dumb, Dumber, Dumbest.* New York: Plume, 1998.

Kutler, Stanley, and Richard M. Nixon, ed. *Abuse of Power: The New Nixon Tapes.* New York: Touchstone Books, 1998.

Liebman, Glenn. *Political Shorts: 1,001 of the Funniest Political One-Liners.* Chicago: Contemporary Books, 1999.

Lippman, Theo. *Spiro Agnew's America.* New York: W. W. Norton, 1972.

Lukas, J. Anthony. *Nightmare: The Underside of the Nixon Years.* Columbus: Ohio University Press, 1999.

Maranis, David, and Michael Weisskopf. *Tell Newt To Shut Up!* New York: Simon & Schuster, 1996.

McCain, John. *Faith of My Fathers: A Family Memoir.* New York: Random House, 1999.

McMullan, Jim. *Hail to the Chief.* Los Angeles: GPG, 1996.

Minutaglio, Bill. *First Son: George W. Bush and the Bush Family Dynasty.* New York: Times Books, 1999.

Morris, Edmund. *Dutch: A Memoir of Ronald Reagan.* New York: Random House, 1999.

Nessen, Ron. *It Sure Looks Different from the Inside.* Chicago: Playboy Press, 1979.

New Republic, The, ed. *Bushisms*. New York: Workman Publishing, 1992.

Olive, David. *Political Babble: The 1,000 Dumbest Things Ever Said by Politicians*. New York: John Wiley & Sons, 1992.

Petras, Ross, and Kathryn Petras. *The Stupidest Things Ever Said by Politicians*. New York: Pocket Books, 1999.

————. *The 365 Stupidest Things Ever Said*. New York: Workman Publishing, 1997.

Posner, Gerald. *Citizen Perot: His Life and Times*. New York: Random House, 1996.

Quigley, Joan. *What Does Joan Say? My Seven Years as White House Astrologer to Nancy and Ronald Reagan*. New York: Birch Lane, 1990.

Ross, Shelley. *Fall from Grace: Sex, Scandal, and Corruption in American Politics from 1702 to the Present*. New York: Ballantine Books, 1988.

Slansky, Paul. *The Clothes Have No Emperor: A Chronicle of the American 80s*. New York: Simon & Schuster, 1989.

Strausbaugh, John. *Alone with the President*. New York: Blast Books, 1993.

Tally, Steve. *Bland Ambition: From Adams to Quayle—the Cranks, Criminals, Tax Cheats, and Golfers who Made It to Vice President*. New York: Harcourt Brace Jovanovich, 1992.

Timberg, Robert. *The Nightingale's Song*. New York: Touchstone Books, 1996.

Udall, Morris K. *Too Funny to Be President*. New York: Henry Holt, 1988.

Who's Who in American Politics 1997–1998. New Providence, NY: Marquis Who's Who, 1998.

Wicker, Tom. *One of Us: Richard Nixon and the American Dream*. New York: Random House, 1991.

Wilson, Will. *Fool for a Client*. (unpublished manuscript), 1999.

Zacks, Richard. *History Laid Bare: Love, Sex, and Perversity from the Ancient Etruscans to Warren G. Harding*. New York: HarperCollins, 1994.

WEB REFERENCE SITES

Official Web sites of various politicians usually only provide limited bio-graphical information along with selected speeches and press releases—bor-ing. Most anti-candidate Internet sites ignore the good dumb stuff in favor of polemics. Below I have listed those sites I found most useful in compiling this book, but if you find any additional good ones, let us know and we'll post them at our own Web site: www.dumbest.com. (Please note that Internet Web sites frequently change their URL addresses.)

For basic biographical information on Congress and the president:
bioguide.congress.gov/biosearch/biosearch.asp
www.capweb.net
www.vote-smart.org

For information on selected politicians:
House of Crooks (www.sit.wisc.edu/~lsfitzge)

For information on presidential candidates:
Skeleton Closet (www.realchange.org)

For information on Gov. George W. Bush
(and one of the most informative political profile sites on the Web):
www.geocities.com/CapitolHill/3750/bushreport.htm

INDEX

DeLay, Tom, 52–54
Delta Kappa Epsilon, 130
Deng Xiaoping, 31
DePauw University, 128
Desperate Journey, 133
Devlin, Daniel F., 100
Dickey, Jay, 101
divorce, 19–20, 22–23, 25, 46, 49, 51, 55, 62, 77, 80, 101, 107, 109, 120, 122, 132–33
"Dixie," 95
Doe, Samuel K., 134
Dole, Bob, 55–58
Dole, Elizabeth "Liddy" Hanford, 55–58
Dole, Phyllis Holden, 55–56
Dornan, Bob, 59–61, 72–74
Dornan, Sallie Hansen, 59, 74
Douglas, Helen Gahagan, 116
Douglas, Melvin, 116
Downey, Thomas, 61
drugs, 17, 27, 38–39, 44, 77, 83, 101, 103, 109, 117, 126, 144, 151, 156
Dukakis, Michael, 57
Duke, Chloe Hardin, 62
Duke, David, 30, 62
Duke University, 56, 114–15, 124
Dunkin' Donuts, 58

Edwards, Edwin, 65
Ehrlichman, John, 117
Eisenhower, Dwight D., 110, 115–16, 141
Electronic Data Systems (EDS), 150, 152
Ellsberg, Daniel, 118
Emory University, 77
environmental issues, 37, 46, 48, 53, 65, 106, 127, 134
Ethiopia, 17
Eureka College, 132
evolution, 52, 102

Fall, Albert Bacon, 93
FBI. *See* Federal Bureau of Investigation
Fantasy Island, 26
federal budget, 53, 79, 131
Federal Bureau of Investigation (FBI), 97, 119, 126, 132, 145
fights, 29, 54, 60–61, 93, 108, 113, 141–42
Finders-Keepers, 64
Finland, 69
fishing, 155
Florida, 43, 75, 98, 103, 108
Flynn, Errol, 132
Flynt, Larry, 22, 101
Follett, Ken, 152
Food Network, 83
football, 57, 66–68, 117, 143
Forbes, Charlie, 93
Forbes, Steve, 20
Ford, Elizabeth "Betty" Bloomer Warren, 27, 66–67, 69
Ford, Gerald, 28, 57, 66–71, 119
Foster, Vince, 33
France, 118, 157
Frank, Barney, 19, 21
Fromme, Lynette Alice "Squeaky," 70
Frost, David, 119

gambling, 65, 93, 115
Garner, Jack, 36
gays, 19, 21, 60–61, 72–76, 97
General Electric, 132, 136
General Motors, 152
George Washington University, 22
Georgetown University, 22, 28
Georgia, 22, 77, 85, 105
Gettysburg College, 124
Gibson, John, 54
Gingrich, Jackie Battley, 77, 79
Gingrich, Marianne Ginther, 77, 79
Gingrich, Newt, 22, 54, 77–80

ABOUT THE AUTHOR

Bill Crawford first got involved in politics as an elementary-school student, when he volunteered for the 1968 George Wallace presidential campaign. If that wasn't dumb enough, he graduated from Phillips Academy, Andover, earned a degree in the study of religion from Harvard University, got an M.B.A. from the University of Texas at Austin, and started writing books. Crawford has written for the *Austin Chronicle, Texas Monthly, Oklahoma Today*, and a number of other publications. He is the author of *Democrats Do the Dumbest Things* (Renaissance, 2000) and co-author of five previous books, including *Stevie Ray Vaughan: Caught in the Crossfire* (Little, Brown, 1993), *Rock Stars Do the Dumbest Things* (Renaissance, 1998), *Movie Stars Do the Dumbest Things* (Renaissance, 1999), and *Border Radio*. Crawford lives in Austin, Texas, with his wife and two children, who all play soccer while he drinks tequila.

ALSO AVAILABLE FROM
RENAISSANCE BOOKS

BOOKS